2651

New Soundings

New Soundings

Essays on Developing Tradition

Edited by STEPHEN PLATTEN
GRAHAM JAMES
and ANDREW CHANDLER

DARTON·LONGMAN + TODD

First published in 1997 by
Darton, Longman and Todd Ltd
1 Spencer Court
140–142 Wandsworth High Street
London SW18 4JJ

ISBN 0–232–52147–6

A catalogue record for this book is available
from the British Library

Phototypeset by Intype London Ltd
Printed and bound in Great Britain by
Redwood Books, Trowbridge, Wiltshire

Contents

Preface

Andrew Chandler

Why, and how, should we talk of tradition? In an age in which we are conscious of unsettling new currents, the language of tradition has provided the words of dispute. Those who report the affairs of Christian life are much given to writing of traditionalists and liberals – those who wish to affirm the claims of the past against change and those who move the argument forward on to new ground. We hear that the credibility of the Christian Church lies in the preservation and true inheritance of a definitive past. We are told that a Church which adapts to different days weakens the truth it inherits. Then we are left to wonder what a Church that lives only in the past can say to a present which seems very different.

Stephen Platten, Graham James and I first sat down to discuss the writing of this book early in 1994. Stephen was then Secretary for Ecumenical Affairs to the Archbishop of Canterbury at Lambeth Palace. Graham, formerly chaplain to the Archbishop, had for two years been Bishop of St Germans. I taught modern history at the universities of Keele and Birmingham. We were, I think, anxious to explore what tradition – if the word itself was viable – should mean to Christians. Was it the repetition of earlier patterns, or the recognition that the past is a story of change, accepting the invitation to develop what we inherit in certain ways? We were encouraged to think that a new volume of essays by Anglican writers of different generations and backgrounds might make a contribution. At various moments over the last hundred years, small clusters of scholars have stepped back from the ongoing life of the Church, viewed its preoccupations, and contributed in such a way to the development of Christian life. This has, perhaps, become something of a tradition in itself.

A book should begin with a claim. It is in the nature of authentic Christian faith that we live and worship as a part of that great fabric of past insight and practice, present ideals and future expectation, which we call the communion of saints. And that community is never static, but always moving, not least because it lives inescapably within a world of unfolding time. We should not assume that a reiteration of past designs shows respect for them and change does not. The value of tradition lies in our belief that we can listen to each other through the ages and move together as a transcendent body of faith. Christian tradition is not an axe to be ground by dogmatists, whose views acquire their clarity by too crude – and too obvious – a selection from the past. It is that sense of wholeness which we try to perceive across time, and in which we find our own place. It is tradition which offers a framework in which to breathe, and an invitation to play our own part in the great theme. Arguably, we live today in a secular culture which believes that freedom to choose and grow is only secured by an absence of inherited, or defining, structures. But in the Church we find that tradition is not essentially about confinement, but about meaningful and lasting creation. It is life given, and life-giving.

Tradition is widely understood as an historical argument. But our sense of history is fragile and complicated, and our past is inevitably difficult to interpret. We cannot argue that tradition offers a linear narrative, or progress, for it is a far more complex matrix of experiences which is difficult to resolve into clear forms. Certainly, it is a mistake to chase after precedents like lawyers. Those who find great statements of belief and set them in stone must acknowledge that such words are themselves expressions, or confirmations, of historical movements. And when we look around we observe that different churches make cardinal truths out of statements that other churches consign to the background of history. Moreover, the story of Christianity is not merely a pageant of self-propelling faith and independent institutional definition. We cannot understand the historical Church if we isolate it from the environment in which it lived and worked. The Christian experience is continually shaped by its engagement with a wider world of different powers, beliefs and values. Now, a credible Christianity which lives at once in past, present and future states is not merely an inward-looking vision of life, but one that requires us to look outwards and listen sensitively.

Such a view of tradition may make us uneasy, but no other can be credible. Christianity is a faith, and our confidence in the Church does not rest on certainty. It rests on the great truth that we may find a sense of identity and direction in that great breadth of experience which is offered to us when we become a part of Christ's body.

The very wholeness of the tradition in which we live certainly demands much of us. Our vision of God calls us to be faithful students of the texts we most cherish, the history we inherit, the words we speak together, the condition of our society, our relationship with other faiths and the new wisdom of scholarship. We invited eight writers, five men and three women, to join with us in the writing of the book. At the beginning of January 1996 we congregated at Bishop's Croft in Birmingham, where we enjoyed the generous hospitality and stimulating companionship of our host, the Bishop of Birmingham. For two days we worshipped together and shared our thoughts, in formal discussions and over meals. And there we felt the different experiences of each writer combine with some liveliness and creative force. This book is the expression of the ideas which were brought to that gathering and explored there. It is written by Christians who are seeking to listen, and respond, to the questions of authority, change and self-identity which we face at the close of the century. The title, *New Soundings*, suggested by Linda Woodhead, recalls that distinguished earlier book, edited by Alec Vidler, to which many of us feel a debt. This, we believed, was a time to look around again.

Notes on Contributors

Arnold Browne is Dean of Chapel and Director of Studies in Theology at Trinity College, Cambridge. He has been a parish priest in the Guildford Diocese and a chaplain in London University. He has specialised in New Testament studies and in counselling psychology.

Andrew Chandler taught Modern History at the Universities of Birmingham and Keele from 1990 to 1996. He is now Director of the George Bell Institute and Senior Research Fellow at the Ecumenical Foundation for Theological Education at Queens, Birmingham.

Grace Davie teaches sociology in the University of Exeter. She is a specialist in the sociology of religion. Her most recent book is *Religion in Britain since 1945: Believing without Belonging*. She is currently preparing a book on religion in Europe. She is the convenor of the International Society for the Sociology of Religion.

Perran Gay is Canon Chancellor of Truro Cathedral and Director of Ministerial Education for the Diocese of Truro. Previously he was the Bishop of Truro's Domestic Chaplain and Diocesan Ecumenical Officer. Before ordination he taught RE in a comprehensive school.

Leslie Houlden is Emeritus Professor of Theology at King's College, London, and the author of numerous books on the New Testament and Christian belief.

Graham James has been Bishop of St Germans in the Diocese of Truro since 1993. His earlier ministry took place in parishes in Peterborough and Welwyn Garden City, then at the Advisory Council for the Church's Ministry before he became Chaplain to the Archbishop of Canterbury.

Philip Lewis is Inter-Faith Adviser to the Bishop of Bradford and lectures at Leeds University Department of Theology and Religious Studies. Previously he spent six years at the ecumenical Christian Study Centre in Pakistan researching Islam and Muslim-Christian relations. His latest book is *Islam in Britain: Religion, Politics and Identity among British Muslims*.

Stephen Platten is Dean of Norwich. He has taught theology and has written in a variety of journals. His most recent book traces the roots of Christian mission in Britain.

David Stancliffe has been Bishop of Salisbury since 1993. Before that he served a curacy in Leeds, was a School Chaplain and then a Director of Ordinands. He was Provost of Portsmouth from 1982 to 1993 and has wide-ranging interests in liturgy, church buildings and music. He is currently Chairman of the Liturgical Commission.

Angela Tilby is an award-winning senior producer of Religious Programmes at BBC North. She joined the BBC in 1973 after reading theology at Cambridge University. She is also an author and reviewer. Her books include *Science and the Soul*, for which she was awarded a John Templeton Foundation prize. She is preparing for ordination in the Diocese of St Albans.

Linda Woodhead is Lecturer in Christian Studies at Lancaster University. She has written numerous articles on theological and ethical topics, as well as on contemporary religion. She is currently completing a book on the rise of alternative post-traditional spirituality in India and the West.

Introduction

Graham James

Back in the 1960s the response of Roman Catholics to the Second Vatican Council revealed how a developing tradition arouses contrasting reactions. Two examples will stand as an illustration of the tension in the theme which this set of essays seeks to address.

On Easter Day 1966 Evelyn Waugh died after attending Mass. Ten days earlier he had written a disconsolate letter to Diana Mosley, lamenting what 'Pope John and his Council' had done to the liturgy. 'I now cling to the Faith doggedly without joy. Churchgoing is a pure duty parade.'[1]

A few days before Christmas in that same year Father Charles Davis announced that he was leaving the Roman Catholic Church. He was a well-known priest and the editor of *The Clergy Review*. For Davis the Second Vatican Council had not gone far enough. It left papal authority securely in place (as was to be demonstrated when Pope Paul VI issued the encyclical *Humanae Vitae*[2] in July 1968). The Roman Catholic Church, declared Davis, was a pseudo-political structure and it would soon break up under the weight of its own contradictions.

Both Waugh and Davis knew they were living in a generation when the Catholic tradition was undergoing change. Their disagreement was profound, but it was the very consciousness of change which created an additional discomfort. For Waugh the tradition had developed, but these further developments were unwelcome. For Davis there was, as the title of his eventual book[3] made clear, a question of conscience in remaining within a tradition, elements of which did not appear to be open to further development at all. Neither despised tradition. Neither

1

denied development. Both felt keenly the impact of a developing tradition, but in different ways. They were not alone.

Within the Church of England in the early 1960s it was not the Second Vatican Council but the publication of *Honest to God*[4] which was the focus of doctrinal change. Even though its author, John Robinson, was an Anglican bishop, the book may have passed without notice were it not for two things. An *Observer* article trailing the book was given the title 'Our Image of God Must Go'. Robinson didn't much care for this iconoclasm but couldn't suggest anything better. Then, secondly, he had already established a controversial reputation as 'the *Lady Chatterley* bishop'. His testimony in the 1960 trial in favour of the open publication of D. H. Lawrence's novel led both to a public rebuke from the Archbishop of Canterbury and to the sort of notoriety that can only result from religion getting mixed up with sex. Robinson seemed to exemplify the New Morality and clearly wanted a New Reformation. So among conservatives and radicals alike there was a consciousness of change and development. The tumult within the Church simply reflected the storms and tempests in wider society. Harold Wilson came into office as Prime Minister promising to harness the white heat of a technological revolution. For those who clung to the security of what they believed was an unchanging tradition, the world seemed to be in melt-down.

A generation on, we live with a legacy from the sixties which cannot be ignored. This book is not about the sixties as such, but many of its contributors were either born in that decade, or grew up in the sixties or began their professional careers at that time. In the nineties we are still conscious of change, yet the optimism of many in the sixties that developments would almost of necessity be for the better has gone. There's a degree of foreboding about the future. The Millennium draws near, and both within the Church and outside it we are not quite sure how to celebrate it or what we should be celebrating. It's partly because we now live in an age which seems torn between the challenge of change and a longing for tradition. We celebrate anniversaries at the drop of a hat, perhaps as a sign of a lack of confidence in our own achievements. Ours is an era which embraces the Internet and virtual reality, yet wants its architecture traditional, its countryside preserved and its heritage conserved. Real bread, real ale and organic vegetables sit on the shelves of supermarkets which in other respects exemplify the changed relationships in contemporary culture. Shopping is now a leisure activity, even a sacred ritual for Sundays. Our supermarkets have aisles; there are processions to the till; the ritual when you get there is precise; and despite the crowds in a supermarket, there is generally a hushed silence. People turn round to stare at the crying child, just as they do in church. The tension between tradition and change is readily observable.

It was not always thus. There have been periods of history, even quite recently, when, within the Christian Church, our understanding of the nature of God and his relationship with the world developed and changed almost imperceptibly. Christians seem most comfortable with a changing tradition when they are largely unaware of it. It is only in recent years, for example, that the decline of belief in the everlasting punishment of the wicked has been recognised. It was in 1864 that 10,906 clergy of the Church of England signed a petition. They did so in response to the publication of *Essays and Reviews*, that seminal but now almost unreadable introduction of biblical criticism into English clerical life, which was published just two years earlier. Those who signed this petition – nearly 60 per cent of the total number of Anglican clergy at the time – wished the world to know that they believed in the inerrancy of Scripture, and because of that, they believed too that the punishment of the wicked, like the life of the righteous, was everlasting. The disintegration of the power of belief in the everlasting punishment of the wicked has been, until recently, a largely unexamined phenomenon.[5] What is unmistakable is that something that was once thought central to Christian belief is now marginal and marginalised. There are still echoes around, of course, as the reception of the Church of England Doctrine Commission's report *The Mystery of Salvation*[6] revealed. But the temper of

3

that report is very different from that which was current in the mid-nineteenth century. It is a sign of a major doctrinal shift which took place speedily but largely unnoticed. The Church has lived with this change by not doing too much to define it.

Yet there are moments when change is recognised, is defined and can even be dated. On 11 November 1992 the General Synod of the Church of England voted in favour of the ordination of women to the priesthood. There can be nothing imperceptible about that sort of change within the Christian tradition. Both the most enthusiastic supporter of the ordination of women and its most determined opponent must interpret this decision within an understanding of how the Christian tradition changes, why it does, and what is encompassed by tradition in any case. The Christian Church is challenged with questions of authority, change and self-identity. These are unavoidable, for none of us live in hermetically sealed worlds where change within another branch of the Christian Church fails to affect us. The Church of England's decision on the ordination of women to the priesthood was one of the factors leading to the Papal Letter on the subject just two years later. That letter declared that the Catholic Church had no authority to change the tradition which it had received on this matter. It is doubtful if it will succeed in closing the debate even within the Roman Catholic Church itself, for the discussion about the nature of tradition, its boundaries and possibilities for development and change, is too well established.

In recent years there has been a growing convergence of previously disparate strands within the Christian tradition generally. Even 50 years ago few Protestants would have read Roman Catholic theology. Papal encyclicals had modest impact outside the Catholic community. Yet in 1993 the publication of Pope John Paul II's *Veritatis Splendor*[7] occasioned a widespread debate about the Church's moral teaching, both within and outside the Roman Catholic Church. Here was teaching within a tradition, and developing it, which was welcome to those who would be otherwise reluctant to acknowledge the authoritative

4

teaching office of the Holy Father. The scholarly ecumenism of recent years has spread beyond the bounds of the academic community and is reflected in the life of the various churches themselves. Liturgical change has added to this convergence of traditions. Charismatic renewal has stirred the previously suspicious into a Spirit-filled recognition of each other's value. Very different religious communities such as those at Taizé and Iona have made an impact far beyond the traditions which have nurtured them. All of us 'own' a great deal more of the wider Christian tradition than we once did. Protestants and Anglicans even find that the Reformation didn't need to happen to revive popular religion in England. Eamon Duffy has told us it was alive and well, after all, in the early sixteenth century.[8]

The issues with which this book deals continue to be debated within the Christian Church, simply because the Christian Church itself continues. The passage of time has presented difficulties for Christians from roughly the end of the first century AD onwards. The very first generation of Christians were waiting for the end. God's coming Kingdom was imminent. Gradually, though, as the eschaton moved steadily into the future, that which was received and was to be handed on (i.e. the Christian tradition) became something of which Christians were conscious. The content and nature of that which was to be handed on from one generation to another became the focus of all the major arguments between Christians, and provided the dynamic for Christianity's own development.

This remains a living question because tradition is lived. If it is lived, it has to be understood and received. And Christianity can only give breath and life to the tradition where there is a spirit and openness to receive it.

The sense of a tradition to be handed on is to be found even in the writings of St Paul. In 1 Corinthians 11:23 he asked the Corinthians to keep faith with the tradition he received from the Lord himself regarding the Eucharist. The authority of that tradition derived from the authority of Christ. It settled an argument, one of the most significant and enduring uses of tradition within Christian history. It

5

is also telling that this Pauline reference should be to the Eucharist, itself a bearer and focus of tradition.

In the Eucharist the Christian community 'recalls', but always in such a way as to make the reality and meaning of Christ's salvific death on the cross present within the action. The Eucharist is a memorial of a past event but also an anticipation of the heavenly banquet. The bread is broken as a sign of Christ's broken body, but Christ is received alive. Where the Church is rooted most in the past it is also directed to the future. The tension this creates is integral to the life of the Church in this provisional time, for the Christian Church on earth always lives in a provisional age, as it awaits the coming of the Kingdom. That's what makes the 'handing on' of tradition important.

The recognition of what is to be handed on is precious, because it is the key not simply to understanding but to salvation. This is what gives the tradition of the apostolic age such authority. It was very early in Christian history that traditionalists emerged who believed that the original faith was given in the apostolic age, and the task of later generations was simply to proclaim, teach, guard and transmit it. Tertullian exemplified this approach in the second century. Innovation was, of necessity, heretical, and the fear was already present that the more distant the apostolic age became, the looser became our hold on the precious truth of the Gospel if it was not guarded with vigilance.

In *The Myth of Christian Beginnings*[9] Robert Wilken illustrates two clear but contrasting features of Christianity down the centuries. He shows how reluctant the tradition has been to give any place to change, while demonstrating the capacity of the tradition to change. It doesn't take an acute observer to notice that late-twentieth-century North American Catholicism is rather different to sixteenth-century Counter-Reformation Catholicism in Italy. Christianity in fifth-century Constantinople bears little superficial resemblance to Irish Presbyterianism in the nineteenth. Both would be shocked if it was suggested that they were in any way unfaithful to the apostolic tradition.

Christian controversy has been focused often between

groups competing over their faithfulness to the apostolic age. The Reformers of the sixteenth century all believed they were returning to a more authentic tradition. Catholic apologists of the period sought to prove them wrong. Both assumed that there was a single authentic apostolic tradition to be found, cherished, preserved and guarded. The Christian faith was rooted in the past. Robert Wilken skilfully shows how hateful was the charge of novelty to the Protestants and Roman Catholics alike. The Reformers claimed to return to a primitive authenticity. The Catholics stressed continuity in the preservation of the apostolic tradition within the institutional Church. Notions of development in doctrine were alien to both traditions.

Gradually, however, the existence of two quite separate ways of viewing a common past hastened the rise of historical consciousness. If you are aware that there is more than one way of regarding Christian history, you recognise that you must be an interpreter of the past. Perhaps we are now in danger of being so conscious of our interpretative role that we think there is no such thing as authentic tradition. That seems to be Wilken's rather bleak conclusion:

> There is no original Christian faith, no native language, no definitive statement of the meaning of Christ for all times. The dialectic of past and present, tradition and innovation, permanence and change, runs through the whole history of Christianity. What is regarded as novel to one generation becomes authoritative tradition to another. Christians have, in their construction of the past, prized antiquity, stability and permanence, but the historical record shows quite another picture... No matter how deeply we probe, how early we extend our search, we will never find an original faith.[10]

It is Wilken's hope that instead of always looking to the past, the Church should look to the future, to the coming Kingdom which Jesus proclaimed. For him perfection lies not in the beginning but at the end. The Christian faith embodies the vision of God and expresses the longing of men and women for something that is yet to be realised but which is promised in Christ. What is 'handed on' is that vision, always imperfect in itself, inevitably incomplete, but leading to a future in which the truth will be revealed.

There is a confidence in such a vision which betrays the decade in which Wilken's book was conceived and written. Published in 1971, it breathes a confidence about the future, a Christian optimism which doesn't quite ring true in the last few years of the Millennium. It is perhaps only at the end of this twentieth century that the impact of significant developments in intellectual life are being absorbed within the Christian tradition, and making an impression upon our understanding of tradition itself.

Religion is intellectually conservative. The fixity of apostolic tradition for so many generations of Christians has not been abandoned in the popular Christian mind. But it has increasingly been held alongside other convictions. It may have been long ago that the majority of Christians came to terms with the theory of evolution (or rather theories, since even our understanding of evolution evolves). The concept whereby the natural order is understood to be in a ceaseless process of change has a greater impact than simply upon the relationship of religion and science. You cannot live within a world marked by change and development without it having an impact upon theological thinking more generally. An age of quarks and gluons is one in which our conception of matter itself loses that stability and solidity which previous generations of Christians associated with the natural order. These are not 'problems' to be reconciled with an inherited religious tradition which is fixed, received and unchangeable. Rather, they form the backdrop of all our thinking.

So Christians who value what we have received from the past, and understand tradition as the living dynamic of Christian life, want to rescue tradition from being seen as a negative, closed system. The authors of this book do not regard tradition as a Christian fossil, full of historical interest and worth analysing so that our origins may be better known. The Christian tradition is lived in the handing over, the communication of the faith from generation to generation. Tradition is a holy communion of faith from one age to another. The difficulty is that ours is an age strangely unknowledgeable about our past, in which a sense of where we have come from culturally, historically, politically and religiously is not very keen. So it's easy to confuse tradition with traditions, those hangovers from the past in which customs are preserved when their meaning has been forgotten.[11] An impatience with the supposed meaninglessness of traditions can generate an unsympathetic response to tradition itself.

Let's take an uncontroversial example. Those women who still feel it appropriate to wear a hat in church (a diminishing but not yet extinct group) are unlikely to be mindful of St Paul's strictures in 1 Corinthians 11 as the grounds for doing so. Paul commends the Corinthians for 'maintaining the tradition I handed on to you' (1 Cor. 11:2) in matters of public worship. He then reminds them that 'a woman brings shame on her head if she prays or prophesies bareheaded' (1 Cor. 11:5). Unlike a man, who is made in God's image and so reflects God's glory, a woman is made out of man and reflects man's glory rather than God's. Her head is to be covered as a sign of the authority under which she lives.

It's doubtful whether many hatted women in church recognise that this is what the custom once signified. The Pauline tradition was, however, powerful enough to deserve reference from the Archbishops of Canterbury and York in 1942 when they put out a joint statement wishing it to be known that 'No woman or girl should hesitate to enter a church (with head) uncovered, nor should any objection to their doing so be raised.' The Archbishops, in arguing their case, simply said that 'St Paul's regulation . . . has long ago fallen out of use.' In itself this was an archiepiscopal recognition of a developing tradition, but not one much commented upon at the time. And why were the Archbishops issuing a statement about such an arcane subject when the country was at war? It was at the request of the President of the Board of Trade, Hugh Dalton. There were problems in keeping the nation's women hatted, and labour and material would be saved if they went hatless. The President of the Board of Trade made no mention of St Paul in his request to the Archbishops.[12]

There are a number of significant points about tradition and traditions which are revealed in this, at first sight, trivial example. The first is the way in which a tradition can continue seemingly unchanged yet gradually come to signify something quite different from its original inspiration or causation. The culture around changes, and so even the most protective traditionalist cannot prevent a well-guarded and well-preserved tradition from conveying a changed meaning.

Stephen Sykes once reflected upon his experience of the Royal Maundy Service in just this way, recognising that, despite the remarkably unchanging tradition of the rite, it could not signify what it once did generations ago, such are the cultural shifts that have taken place.[13] Even within the rite itself, of course, the presence of clergy with towels ritually wrapped around their waists is a reminder of an even older tradition when the monarch actually washed the feet of the poor. And that, in turn, reflected an older tradition still found in the Gospels, and the origin and foundation of this act of humility and service on the part of the sovereign. However the Royal Maundy Service is interpreted today, its development as a tradition is as unmistakable as the way in which its relationship to our culture has changed. So too for the hatted women in church. In the late twentieth century the hat signifies respectability and gentility rather than subordination. An unchanged tradition may come to convey a radically different message.

The second point about the covered heads of the women is the way we see the distinction between tradition and traditions already reflected in the Scriptures themselves. Paul hands on particular traditions, but within the context of the tradition of being 'in Christ'. 1 Corinthians 11 concludes with the bald statement, 'The other matters I will settle when I come' (1 Cor. 11:34). We do not know what these matters were, except that coming at the end of Paul's peroration about the conduct of public worship, they must have been related to that subject. Clearly there are primary and secondary matters. Some things concerning worship are more pressing than others. One of the tests of being 'in Christ' is discerning the relative importance of what is to be handed on. There are 'things indifferent', and Anglicanism in particular has been keen, from Hooker onwards, to recognise this.[14]

Thirdly, already in Paul's letters we observe a determination to symbolise continuity by means of the handing on of tradition. Paul's writings will become Christian Scripture and so a symbol of continuity in themselves; the sacraments have already been established as the bearers of continuity; the ministerial priesthood will gradually emerge to guard and guarantee continuity of belief and practice; the Creeds will eventually summarise that which is to be 'handed on' as the deposit of faith. But all these bearers of Christian tradition can become shells without living creatures within, fossils on the beach, symbols of a lost continuity. Continuity in the Christian faith can only be guaranteed by a readiness to innovate. Stephen Sykes expressed it thus:

> we must resist the package offered us by traditionalists, who assert that their mere preservation guarantees the continuous identity of the Church. On the contrary, it is only when the deposit is supported by inventiveness . . . that the Christian faith will be represented with the wholeness it requires in our present age.[15]

The essayists in this book believe there is a temptation to dismiss the need to reverence tradition in the Christian Church, and to mistake it for an unwarranted affection for dated customs. We want to resist that temptation. But we do so not to encourage a conservative backlash or a narrow traditionalism. A reverence for tradition may alert us to the impact of a changing culture on the symbols of Christian continuity. It encourages us to innovate so that what the tradition signifies is still shaped by Christians themselves rather than by the prevailing, and possibly non-Christian or post-Christian, culture. A changing culture is reflected in some of the chapters in this book. The presence of different faith communities alongside Christianity in Great Britain; the development of sociological methods as a means of interpreting religious life; the rise of feminist perspectives: these are innovations, and their impact upon our understanding of the Christian tradition is considered. But this

11

is no narrowly contemporary agenda. A living Christian tradition engages with the Scriptures; the writings of the Fathers; the vision of God experienced by Christians in previous ages and very different societies: these too are considered here. We seek not to define tradition narrowly for, as this Introduction illustrates, it is both dangerously and creatively elusive. But we are convinced that it is only by taking tradition seriously and living within it that Christians will make any new soundings at all.

Notes to Introduction

1 Mark Amory (ed.), *The Letters of Evelyn Waugh* (Weidenfeld & Nicholson, 1980), p. 639.
2 *Humanae Vitae* was the encyclical issued by Paul VI reaffirming the ban on artificial forms of contraception, and ignoring the conclusions of the special commission he had established to advise him.
3 Charles Davis, *A Question of Conscience* (Hodder & Stoughton, 1967).
4 John A. T. Robinson, *Honest to God* (SCM Press, 1963).
5 The most comprehensive treatment of this subject is found in G. R. Rowell, *Hell & the Victorians* (OUP, 1974).
6 *The Mystery of Salvation* (Church House Publishing, 1995).
7 *Veritatis Splendor*, Encyclical Letter addressed by Pope John Paul II to all the bishops of the Catholic Church regarding certain fundamental questions of the Church's moral teaching (Libreria Editrice Vaticana, 1993).
8 Eamon Duffy, *The Stripping of the Altars* (Yale University Press, 1992). In addition, Christopher Haigh, *English Reformations* (OUP, 1993), offers another perspective (and less polemical than Duffy) on popular religion in sixteenth-century England.
9 Robert Wilken, *The Myth of Christian Beginnings* (New York, Doubleday, 1971, and London, SCM Press, 1979).
10 Ibid., p. 185.
11 See George Guiver, *Faith in Momentum* (SPCK, 1990), especially ch. 4.
12 For an account of this episode, see William Temple, *Some Lambeth Letters*, ed. F. S. Temple (OUP, 1963), pp. 33–5.
13 Stephen Sykes, 'Guard the Deposit' in *Tradition and Unity*, Sermons published in honour of Robert Runcie, ed. D. Cohn-Sherbok (London, Bellew, 1991), pp. 150–55.
14 As reflected in Perran Gay's essay in this book, and in such books as *The Study of Anglicanism*, ed. Sykes and Booty (SPCK, 1988).
15 Sykes, op. cit., p. 154.

1 Yesterday and Today and Forever: The Dynamic of Scripture

Arnold Browne

Continuity and change

THE FAITH WHICH IS REVEALED IN THE HOLY SCRIPTURES
It is characteristic of Christianity to acknowledge the fundamental role of the Bible in our knowledge of God. However
varied the methods they use and the results they reach, it is
evident that all Christians find in the Bible the source and
the standard of their beliefs and practices. Whether it is
conservative or radical, it is in its appeal to the Scriptures
that a theology claims to be Christian.

All the clergy of the Church of England declare their
'belief in the faith which is revealed in the Holy Scriptures',[1]
but it must be admitted that some accuse others of 'playing
fast and loose with the plain teaching of the Bible', or of
taking up positions which represent 'a departure from
Scripture'. However, it would be a tragedy if 'biblical' were
to be reduced to a party slogan, and it is well worth
returning to the Scriptures themselves. In particular, they
challenge us to consider the relationship between continuity and change, to listen to different answers from a
variety of voices, and to recognise that God may address us
more graciously through the conversation of a community
than in a monologue.

THE GOD WHO WAS AND IS AND IS TO COME
To grow in knowledge of God is to be caught up into the
dynamic process of the fulfilment of his promise. From

13

the Pentateuch to Revelation the promise remains: 'I will take you as my people, and I will be your God' (Exod. 6:7); 'He will dwell with them as their God; they will be his people' (Rev. 21:3). Jews and Christians alike recognise that this process has witnessed both continuity and change, and that the claims of the old and of the new can be found in close conjunction. One passage from the Pentateuch puts the point emphatically: 'God also spoke to Moses and said to him: "I am the Lord [*Yahweh*]. I appeared to Abraham, Isaac, and Jacob as God Almighty [*El Shaddai*], but by my name The Lord [*Yahweh*] I did not make myself known to them" ' (Exod. 6:2f). It is the God of his ancestors who has spoken to Moses, and yet they did not know God by his name, *Yahweh* – 'I am who I am and I will be whatever I will be'. And so the promise is more fully realised: 'I will take you as my people, and I will be your God' (Exod 6:7). Equally emphatic in the New Testament is the opening of Hebrews: 'Long ago God spoke to our ancestors in many and various ways by the prophets, but in these last days he has spoken to us by a Son' (Heb. 1:1f), where again the claim to the new is set in the context of the claim to the old.[2] The longest single quotation of the Jewish Scriptures in the earliest Christian writings, which came in time to be bound together as the Old and New Testaments, is the prophecy in the 'old' Scriptures of the 'new' covenant (testament) with the house of Israel (Jer. 31:31–4, quoted in Heb. 8:8–12).

The dynamic of the promise, 'I will take you as my people, and I will be your God,' indicates that our attention to the past, the present, and the future will enable us to grow both in knowledge of 'him who is and who was and who is to come' (Rev. 1:4; cf. 1:8; 4:8) and in understanding of our identity as his people. Psychotherapists may help their clients towards self-understanding by focusing on the past in psychodynamic regression to childhood, or on the present with person-centred work on the 'here and now', or on the future by exploring the 'personal construct' by which events are anticipated and predicted. The Scriptures reveal who God is and who his people are in relation to the past, the present, and the future. Although there is a remarkable interweaving of the three tenses, we can explore the patterns by beginning with each tense in its turn.

From the past

THE LORD LIVES WHO BROUGHT ISRAEL OUT OF EGYPT

It is particularly at times of crisis that the need to affirm continuity in change is most acute. It was during the Babylonian exile in the sixth century BC that priestly scholars struggled to spell out the promise inherent in Israel's traditional rituals for a generation which was losing hope for the future. To their concern for the present significance of past sources we owe the passage from Exodus considered above, and we can understand their focusing on Moses as one whose new experience more fully explained the old. It is likely that these priestly scholars gave its present shape to the Torah. They look to the past and to the preservation of their source material. For example, they incorporate old explanations of the sabbath (Gen. 2:2f), dietary laws (Gen. 9:4), and circumcision (Gen. 17:9–14), finding a renewal of the divine promise of blessing by bringing alive Israel's ritual and religious observance.

There are, of course, different ways of bringing the past to life, as can be seen by a comparison of Deuteronomy 24:1–4 with Jeremiah 3:1–5.[3] Both passages preserve a law forbidding a husband to remarry his divorced wife if she has subsequently married and divorced someone else. In Deuteronomy the application is strictly legal and individual, whereas in Jeremiah the application is spiritual and national. Perhaps influenced by Hosea's metaphor of God's marriage to his people (Hos. 2:2–15) and deeply troubled at their participation in false religion, Jeremiah describes Israel and Judah as God's wife who has left him and 'has played the whore with many lovers' (Jer. 3:1). In the law of Deuteronomy the first husband 'is not permitted to take her again to be his wife after she has been defiled' (Deut. 24:4), but Jeremiah rephrases the regulations as rhetorical questions: 'If a man divorces his wife and she goes from him and becomes another man's wife, will he return to her? Would not such a land be greatly polluted?' and adds, 'and would

15

you return to me?, says the Lord' (Jer. 3:1). 'No!' must be the law's answer, and yet Jeremiah's message is that this husband will return to his estranged wife if she will return in repentance to him. Jeremiah is not seeking to change the law as it affects individuals, but he is making new use of old material, and he is using the tension created by holding together continuity and change to the very full: 'and would you return to me?, says the Lord.'

A significant aspect of the correlation between old and new is that their relative importance may be dramatically reversed. The book of Jeremiah presents the exodus from Egypt as central to Israel's faith (Jer. 2:6; 7:22, 25; 11:4, 7; 34:13). After the fall of Jerusalem it seems that Jeremiah remained in Judah, but some of those who were exiled to Babylon considered his message in their situation, and by doing so they contributed to the editing of the book. This community used the exodus as an image of return from captivity, making the startling statement that 'it shall no longer be said, "As the Lord lives who brought the people of Israel up out of the land of Egypt" but "As the Lord lives who brought the people of Israel up out of the land of the north" ' (Jer. 16:14f; cf. 23:7f). It does not seem that the return from exile ever replaced the exodus from Egypt in the people's confessional statements about their God, but the prophecy in Jeremiah of 'a new covenant with the house of Israel and with the house of Judah' (Jer. 31:31–4; cf. Ezek. 16:60; 37:26) subsequently played an important part in the discussion of the relationship between continuity and change, and in particular of whether the new enacts and reinforces the old, or whether the old is exceeded and replaced by the new.

Not all appeals to the past are what they seem. 'Consider those giant, Gothic, foreboding castles, with their towers, their battlements, and their gatehouses, which were built by many land-owners across the length and breadth of the British Isles,' says David Cannadine of these late eighteenth- and early nineteenth-century constructions. 'In fact, they were elaborate and flamboyant exercises in parvenu self-concealment.'[4] We are well warned, and indeed it is possible to find written traces of such parvenu self-concealment within the pages of the Scriptures themselves.

2 Chronicles 35:1–19 expands the earlier account in 2 Kings 23:21–3 of King Josiah's celebration of the Passover at the renewal of the covenant. The Chronicler gives the Levites prominence in his account. They are assigned to 'each division of an ancestral house', and it is they who kill and skin the lambs, while the priests dash the blood. The Levites assist the priests by preparing for them the burnt offerings, and the Levites also cook the paschal lambs and carry them to the people. None of these functions of the Levites has any basis in the Pentateuch, where the slaughter and roasting of the Passover lambs is a strictly lay ritual (Exod. 12:1ff). The Chronicler has previously suggested that the involvement of Levites in the Passover ceremonies began as a temporary expedient: 'the Levites had to slaughter the Passover lamb for everyone who was not clean' (2 Chr. 30:17), but now he seems to describe an established practice and says that they are 'acting according to the word of the Lord by Moses' (35:6) and indeed 'as it is written in the book of Moses' (35:6).

Such can be the force of the appeal to the past that we have found the Chronicler transforming new practice into old law. The prophet Amos does not take that step, but it is fascinating to note that he supports his critique of present sacrifice with the divine question: 'Did you bring me sacrifices in the wilderness, O house of Israel?' (Amos 5:25; see also Jer. 7:22). Amos' assumption that in the those first years after the exodus there were no sacrificial offerings is a striking contradiction of the Pentateuchal account (Exod. 19 – Num. 10), and like the Chronicler he demonstrates the tendency, so familiar in religious traditions, to conceive an ideal past into which can be placed the distinctive beliefs and practices of the present. There are many such examples to warn us that in ancient Israel as in modern Britain, things are not always what they seem.

THE LAW CAME LATER

Both for Paul and for the writer of Hebrews the development of a contrast between old and new covenants is an aspect of their claim to establish the new by an appeal to the old. Jeremiah's prophecy of 'a new covenant' (Jer. 31:31–4) is quoted at length in Hebrews (Heb. 8:8–12; cf. 9:15; 10:16f; 12:24). Paul, writing some years earlier, also echoes Jeremiah's 'new covenant'. In 1 Corinthians he says that he has handed on what he has received from the Lord: that 'he took the cup also, after supper, saying "This cup is the new covenant in my blood" ' (1 Cor. 11:23–6; cf. Luke 22:20), and in 2 Corinthians he defends his apostleship: 'our competence is from God, who has made us competent to be ministers of a new covenant, not of letter but of spirit' (2 Cor. 3:6). Both Paul and Hebrews go further than Jeremiah in pursuing the idea of 'a new covenant' to the point of speaking also of 'the old covenant' (2 Cor. 3:14; cf. Heb. 8:13), the first or former covenant (Heb. 8:7, 13; 9:1, 15, 18; 10:9), which is now 'set aside' (2 Cor. 3:7, 11, 14) as 'obsolete' (Heb. 8:13; cf. 10:9).

Paul and Hebrews develop a series of comparisons between the old Sinai covenant and the new covenant in Christ, emphasising the contrast between what is temporary and what is permanent, and above all between death and life. Paul insists that 'the letter kills but the spirit gives life' (2 Cor. 3:6; cf. Gal. 3:21; Rom. 8:2), and Hebrews says: 'the former priests were many in number, because they were prevented by death from continuing in office; but he holds his priesthood permanently, because he continues forever' (Heb. 7:23f).

In Galatians, Paul strenuously maintains that his Gentile converts should not be asked 'to live like Jews' (Gal. 2:14). In particular they should not be compelled to practice 'the works of the law' (Gal. 2:16; 3:2, 5, 10), such as circumcision (5:2–12; 6:12–15), dietary laws (2:12; 4:17), and sabbath observance (4:10), which were commonly mentioned by Paul's pagan contemporaries as distinguishing features of Judaism. Although no great admirer of Judaism, the Roman historian Tacitus is prepared at least to concede that the rites introduced by Moses 'have the defence of antiquity' (*Histories* 5.5.1). Paul, in arguing his case, appeals to an even greater antiquity, moving back from 'the old covenant' of the law, given through Moses on Mount Sinai, to God's earlier promise to Abraham. He insists that 'the scripture, foreseeing that God would justify the Gentiles by faith, declared the gospel beforehand to Abraham, saying, "All the Gentiles shall be blessed in you." For this reason, those who believe are blessed with Abraham who believed' (Gal. 3:8f; cf. Rom. 4:1ff). The law 'which came four hundred and thirty years later' does not nullify the earlier promise (Gal. 3:17). It also seems that Paul turned the tables on his opponents who stressed the importance of the physical, and who may well have informed the Galatians of the tradition that of Abraham's two sons it was Isaac who symbolised the Jews and Ishmael the Gentiles. By an allegorical reading of Genesis, a method of interpretation familiar particularly to those students of the Jewish Scriptures who used the translation into Greek,[5] Paul argues that instead it is Ishmael, 'the child of the slave', who stands for the slavery of the flesh whereas Isaac, 'the child of the free woman', stands for the freedom of the Spirit (Gal. 4:21–31, using Gen. 16; 21).

Paul moved back into the past, from the law given to Moses to the promise made to Abraham, and Hebrews makes a similar move backwards from Moses' brother Aaron to 'King Melchizedek of Salem, priest of the Most High God', who met Abraham and blessed him (Heb. 7:1, recalling Gen. 14:17–20). The straightforward point is that Melchizedek is the first priest mentioned in the Scriptures, both the first in the historical record and, significantly for those readers trained in its study, the first in the sacred text. The Scriptures therefore recognise a priesthood even older than Aaron's 'levitical priesthood', which is associated with the old covenant and its law (Heb. 7:11f; cf. 9:1). Jesus, belonging to the royal tribe of Judah rather than to the priestly tribe of Levi, could not be a priest like Aaron (Heb. 7:13f; 8:4). However, Jesus is the royal priest like Melchizedek, the one of whom the Psalm says: 'You are a priest forever, according to the order of Melchizedek' (Ps. 110:4, quoted in Heb. 5:6; 7:17, 21). Less straightforward is the author's use of an interpretative rule which would have been familiar to his contemporaries who studied the Jewish Scriptures. Because the sacredness of the text was stressed

19

even to the point of being able to argue from its silence, it could be claimed that what is not mentioned in the Torah does not exist.[6] This is why he can say of Melchizedek: 'having neither beginning of days nor end of life, but resembling the Son of God, he remains a priest forever' (Heb. 7:3). The essential contrast is between the old covenant, with its priests who die, and the new covenant, with its priest who continues forever (Heb. 7:23f). There is an undoubted claim to change: 'For when there is a change in the priesthood, there is necessarily a change in the law as well' (Heb. 7:12); but at the same time there is a claim to continuity in that the Scriptures recognise a priesthood older than the levitical priesthood and indeed superior to it, above all in the difference between those who are mortal and the one who lives (Heb. 7:8). The one who 'remains a priest forever' is the Son of God, for in this appeal to antiquity Melchizedek remains only on the page of Scripture.

We may struggle with their exegetical methods, but we can understand that for Paul and for the writer of Hebrews the language of old and new covenants expresses both continuity and change, and we can see that the proclamation of the new can be expressed as a movement even further into the past than the old.

BECAUSE OF YOUR HARDNESS OF HEART

In the book of Jeremiah, the element that is 'new' in the prophecy of the covenant which 'will not be like the covenant that I made with their ancestors' (Jer. 31:32) is in the promise: 'I will put my law within them and I will write it on their hearts' (31:33). There is in these words no promise of a new law or rejection of the old. Within Judaism there was an ongoing discussion of the role of the law in the age to come, and the law of the Messiah was typically seen as the law of Moses, which 'should not only be in force in the Messianic Age, but should be better studied and better observed than ever before.'[7] The Jews who belonged to the Qumran sect, which is known to us from the Dead Sea Scrolls, described themselves as 'members of the New Covenant'.[8] The group's primary method of interpreting

Scripture is to apply its words directly to contemporary events and people, and it seems that they regarded themselves as the faithful remnant of Israel. It is clear that their claim to interpret and observe the law of Moses correctly is by no means a claim to live by a new law: 'therefore a man shall bind himself by oath to return to the Law of Moses, for in it all things are strictly defined.'[9]

In the New Testament we find that it is possible to follow Jesus as Messiah without setting aside the law of Moses. In Acts 21:20 it is said that the many thousands of believers among the Jews 'are all zealous for the law', and it is perhaps more significant that the letter of James, perhaps to be associated with the Early Church in Jerusalem, combines 'the faith of our glorious Lord Jesus Christ' (Jas. 2:1; cf. 1:1) with the demands of 'the whole law' (2:10). James, like Paul, recognises that 'the whole law' is indivisible. This is frequently expressed in Jewish literature, most movingly in the account in 4 Maccabees of the martyrdom of Eleazar, urged by the tyrant Antiochus 'to save yourself by eating pork' (4 Macc. 5:6). In refusing, Eleazar says: 'Do not suppose that it would be a petty sin if we were to eat defiling food; to transgress the law in matters either small or great is of equal seriousness, for in either case the law is equally despised' (4 Macc. 5:19–21). Paul urges that the Galatians should not submit to circumcision because to do so would oblige them 'to obey the entire law' (Gal. 5:3). However, James urges his readers not to sin by showing favour to the rich: 'For whoever keeps the whole law but fails in one point has become accountable for all of it' (Jas. 2:10). Paul (Gal. 5:14; Rom. 13:9) and James (Jas. 2:8), like Jesus and Rabbi Akiba (d. AD 132),[10] quote Leviticus 19:18, 'you shall love your neighbour as yourself' in summarising the law. Paul, who uses the unity of the law as an argument *against* circumcision, may see 'love your neighbour' as the new 'law of Christ' (Gal. 6:2; cf. 1 Cor. 9:21); but James, who uses the unity of the law as an argument *for* welcoming the poor, sees 'love your neighbour' as the key to keeping the old law of Moses.[11] Paul argues that Jesus' death and resurrection deal with 'the curse of the law' to bring 'the blessing of Abraham' (Gal. 3:13f); but James, who does not

21

mention the death and resurrection of Jesus, remains content with the belief, which was fundamental for the rabbis, that in the end 'mercy triumphs over judgement' (Jas. 2:13).[12]

From the evidence of Acts and James, it seems that E. P. Sanders is right to say that 'nothing which Jesus said or did which bore on the law led his disciples after his death to disregard it.'[13] Indeed, it is most likely that Matthew's Gospel was written for a community of Jewish Christians which continued to observe the entire law, now intensified in the Messianic Age: 'For truly I tell you, until heaven and earth pass away, not one letter, not one stroke of a letter, will pass from the law until all is accomplished' (Matt. 5:18).[14]

Sanders argues that any convincing depiction of the historical Jesus should relate him both to his Jewish context and to the movement he initiated which eventually broke with Judaism,[15] thus seeing him as a focal point of the developmental process of continuity and change. Jesus' own attitude to the law can best be understood in terms of this dynamic – for example, in his teaching on divorce:

> Some Pharisees came, and to test him they asked, 'Is it lawful for a man to divorce his wife?' He answered them, 'What did Moses command you?' They said, 'Moses allowed a man to write a certificate of dismissal and to divorce her.' But Jesus said to them, 'Because of your hardness of heart he wrote this commandment for you. But from the beginning of creation, "God made them male and female" [quoting Gen. 1:27; 5:2]. "For this reason a man shall leave his father and mother and be joined to his wife, and the two shall become one flesh" [quoting Gen. 2:24]. So they are no longer two, but one flesh. Therefore what God has joined together let no one separate' (Mark 10:2–9; cf. Matt. 19:3–8).

It is highly probable that both the definition of remarriage as adultery (Matt. 5:31f; 19:9; Mark 10:10–12; Luke 16:18) and the criticism of divorce by appeal to the book of Genesis preserve something very like Jesus' original teaching.[16] Although nothing Jesus says here would lead anyone to disobey the law, there is nevertheless the suggestion that the Mosaic dispensation of commandments written 'because of your hardness of heart' is inadequate. In looking back to 'the beginning of creation', Jesus seems also to look forward to a new age when, in Ezekiel's words, God 'will remove from your body the heart of stone and give you a heart of flesh' (Ezek. 36:26; cf. 11:19).

Jesus himself does not suggest that the law should be broken, but he does indicate the inadequacy of the Mosaic regulations. It is easy to see how such an attitude could be developed either in the direction of a stricter interpretation of the law or in the direction of an abandonment of the law, and we find both these developments within the New Testament.

Matthew presents Jesus as the Messiah who interprets and intensifies the demands of the law, particularly in the Sermon on the Mount. In Matthew 5:21–48, by a series of contrasts between what 'you have heard' and what 'I say to you', Jesus indicates that the commandments must not only be observed but must also be more strictly interpreted: do not kill and do not be angry, do not commit adultery and do not look on someone else with lust (Matt. 5:21f, 27f). The law may of itself be inadequate, but it is to be more strictly interpreted rather than to be set aside. The NRSV gives Matthew 5:21–48 the misleading heading 'Jesus' Teaching Alters the Law', but Matthew's own introduction in 5:17–20 makes clear that the issue is not the alteration but rather the interpretation of the law:

> Whoever breaks one of the least of these commandments, and teaches others to do the same, will be called least in the kingdom of heaven; but whoever does them and teaches them will be called great in the kingdom of heaven. For I tell you, unless your righteousness exceeeds that of the scribes and Pharisees, you will never enter the kingdom of heaven (Matt. 5:19f).

For Mark, on the other hand, 'the Son of Man is lord even of the Sabbath' (Mark 2:28), and Jesus is presented as challenging the law itself. When Matthew's Jesus explains to the disciples his saying that 'it is not what goes into the mouth that defiles a person, but it is what comes out of the mouth that defiles' (Matt. 15:11; cf. Mark 7:15), he opposes nothing in the law. Matthew's version of the dispute is not about dietary laws but about a practice not required by the law: 'to eat with unwashed hands does not defile' (Matt. 15:20). However, Mark's Jesus explains the same saying by telling his disciples that indeed food 'cannot defile', thus setting aside what is written in the law:

> He said to them, 'Then do you also fail to understand? Do you not see that whatever goes into a person from outside cannot defile, since it enters, not the heart but the stomach, and goes out into the sewer?' (Thus he declared all foods clean) (Mark 7:18f).

Had Jesus himself already declared all foods clean, then it would be difficult to understand Peter's reluctance in Acts to kill and eat: 'By no means, Lord; for I have never eaten anything that is profane or unclean' (Acts 10:14), or Paul's argument with him over this issue (Gal. 2:11–14). It is also significant that, in arguing that all food is clean, Paul points to the authority of the risen Lord rather than to any known words of Jesus: 'I know and am persuaded in the Lord that nothing is unclean in itself' (Rom. 14:14).

Both the tradition of Matthew and that of Mark are understandable if Jesus taught not that the law could be disregarded but that it did not go far enough. Jesus himself is the focal point both of continuity and of change. The Gospel of Matthew comes from a Jewish Christian community which stresses the former, but Mark is shaped by the concerns of Gentile Christians and stresses the latter. It is possible that Matthew belongs to a Jewish Christian tradition which we know survived for nearly 400 years, observing the law of Moses as interpreted by Jesus, the messianic prophet like Moses (Deut. 18:15). Mark certainly represents the dominant Christian tradition, which gradually separated from Judaism, no longer seeing the law as the focal point of God's revelation and of his people's identity. That dietary laws are set aside can be seen as important teaching for Christians of Mark's day, as a vital message consistent with Jesus' attitude to interpretations of the law which divided Jews from one another in his day. But Mark goes further in saying that it was Jesus himself who 'declared all foods clean'. Here we notice once more the tendency to place the distinctive practices of the present into the past, and to see what were later developments as already achieved in the time of Jesus. But the diversity of the New Testament response to Jesus serves to remind us once more that things are not always what they seem.

For the present

THUS SAYS THE LORD

Although we have noticed the power of the appeal to the past, it is very frequently the case that there are new words for new times. Whereas the Chronicler turned a new role for the Levites into an old law, Ezekiel announces a change in their status as a divine oracle in the present: 'thus says the Lord God.' The Levites are to be demoted, in punishment for idolatry (Ezek. 44:9–16). Far from idealising the past, Ezekiel regards Israel as corrupt and rebellious from the beginning: 'you were abhorred on the day you were born' (Ezek. 16:5; cf. 20:1–8). He quotes and disputes the people's proverbs,[17] and in antithesis to 'the parents have eaten sour grapes and the children's teeth are set on edge' affirms: 'it is only the person who sins that shall die' (Ezek. 18:1–4), in contrast also to the covenant punishments 'to the third and fourth generation of those who reject me' (Exod. 20:5).

The portrayal of the prophets as messengers places the emphasis on God's word for his people *today*: 'The words of Amos' are: 'Thus says the Lord' (Amos 1:1, 3). Sometimes the new word transforms the old. Malachi's criticism of the priests in the post-exilic temple (Mal. 1:6—2:9) recalls all the key terms of the priestly blessing in the book of Numbers (Num. 6:23–7).[18] But now the message is not 'The Lord bless you and keep you; the Lord make his face to shine upon you, and be gracious to you' (Num. 6:24f), but 'I will rebuke your offspring, and spread dung on your faces, the dung of your offerings, and I will put you out of my presence' (Mal. 2:3). At other times changed circumstances allow old words to be used with new meaning. In his distress Job remembers Psalm 8 only to parody its wonderment at God's concern for humanity: 'What are human beings, that you make so much of them, that you set your mind on them, visit them every morning, test them every moment?' (Job 7:17f; see Ps. 8:4), adding: 'Will you not look away from me for a while?' (Job 7:19). The effect of the parody is similar to the reflection in Ecclesiastes on the righteous, who are in the hand of God: 'whether it is love or hate one does not know' (Eccles. 9:1). That the New Testament can in its turn use Job as a rather surprising example of patience in suffering (Jas. 5:1–11) is a reminder that we best understand the dynamic process of God's promise of his presence by holding together the old words and their new applications.

JESUS AND THE SPIRIT

Paul describes himself as handing on the Church's tradition – both its Gospel of Christ, which he himself had received (1 Cor. 15:3–8), and its memories of Jesus (1 Cor. 7:10f; 9:14; 11:23–6). As he hands it on, he makes his own contribution. He defends his particular understanding of good news for Gentile converts by appeal to his inclusion among those to whom the risen Lord appeared: 'I received it through a revelation of Jesus Christ' (Gal. 1:12, 15f; cf. 1 Cor. 9:1; 15:8). He also offers his own comments and interpretations on the only three occasions when he refers to the words of Jesus.

In 1 Corinthians 7:10f, Paul hands on the Lord's 'commandment' that couples should not divorce, but he adds that, although he would prefer there to be no separation, in the case of a believer whose unbelieving partner leaves the marriage, 'the brother or sister is not bound.' It is worth noting that Matthew adds to the prohibition of divorce: 'except on the ground of unchastity' (Matt. 5:32; cf. 19:9). Whereas Paul explicitly interprets Jesus' teaching for the present circumstances of converted Gentiles, Matthew's interpretation for his community appears as a concession from Jesus within the context of an intensification of the demands of the law.

In 1 Corinthians 9:14, Paul acknowledges that 'the Lord commanded that those who proclaim the gospel should get their living by the gospel' (see Matt. 10:10; Luke 10:7). However, Paul says that he has made no use of this right. In other words, he has chosen to ignore one of the two 'commandments' of Jesus to which he refers. Although, as he says, both the law and the Lord agree on this matter, Paul's present need to defend himself as preaching the Gospel 'free of charge' (1 Cor. 9:18) takes precedence.

In 1 Corinthians 11:23–6, it seems that the words, 'Do this, as often as you drink it, in remembrance of me,' found in Luke but not in Matthew or Mark,[19] had already been added to Jesus' words at the Last Supper in the worship of the Early Church. Paul adds his own interpretative note: 'For as often as you eat this bread and drink the cup, you proclaim the Lord's death until he comes.' Given the careful distinction between his and Jesus' words and opinions in the earlier passages, it would be wrong to imagine that Paul intends his interpretation to be taken as part of what he received 'from the Lord', either from the Church's tradition about Jesus or by a revelation from the risen Christ.

In the Pastoral letters, young widows are instructed to 'marry, bear children, and manage their households, so as to give the adversary no occasion to revile us' (1 Tim. 2:14). It may be that Paul, who once advised single women not to marry and suggested that widows should not remarry (1 Cor. 7:25–39), again has new words in new circumstances. However, it is difficult to imagine that Paul, who believed that 'the present form of this world is passing away' (1 Cor. 7:31), could be quite as concerned as the author of the first letter to Timothy with being 'well thought of by outsiders' (1 Tim. 3:7). If, as seems likely, the Pastoral letters are pseudonymous, then we have an example of one line of development in the post-Pauline churches, one moving in a less rather than a more radical direction, claiming for itself the authority of Paul.

The present work of the Spirit is an important theme in the book of Acts, which describes the expansion of the Early Church. The community in Jerusalem first includes only Jews and proselytes (Acts 2:5, 10). It is then thrown outwards to embrace Samaritans (8:1ff) and God-fearers (8:27; 10:2), then Gentiles from Antioch (10:20; 13:1–3) and as far as Rome (28:16). At each stage the Spirit confirms the development: as for the Jews on the day of Pentecost (2:1ff), so, in due time, for the Samaritans (8:17), the God-fearers (10:44ff) and other Gentiles (19:6). The gift and signs of the Spirit are

27

taken by Peter as the present expression of the will of God: 'If then God gave them the same gift that he gave us when we believed in the Lord Jesus Christ, who was I that I could hinder God?' (11:17; cf. 15:8f, 28). Despite its rather schematised account of agreements, there is evidence in Acts, and rather more in the letters of Paul, that this process of continuity and change was also one of conflict and division. We have seen that within the Early Church there were different attitudes to the law, and there were also different attitudes to the temple. In Acts, Stephen attacks the temple as essentially idolatrous: the direct connection made between the idols made in the wilderness, 'the works of their hands' (7:42), and the temple 'made with human hands' (7:48) is remarkable. But also in Acts, Paul is arrested in the temple on his final visit to Jerusalem. He is there undergoing a rite of purification in order to satisfy those Jewish Christians who were zealous for the law (21:17–30; cf. 24:17f). Within Judaism there was a minority of Greek-speaking Jews who abhorred the bloody reality of the temple and its sacrifices,[20] and it may be that the dispute in Acts between Greek-speaking and Aramaic-speaking Jewish Christians (i.e. Hellenists and Hebrews) involved different attitudes to the temple, and perhaps to those God-fearers who could worship only in its outer court. It is possible that the disagreement over 'the daily distribution of food' could have involved the question of the admission of Gentile God-fearers to the 'tables' (6:1f).[21] Although assessing Jesus' attitude to the temple is 'extremely complicated and controversial',[22] it seems that at least the Hebrews among his followers were happy to continue to worship there after his death and resurrection (2:46; 3:1; 5:12–16). Stephen, a Hellenist, accuses those who worship in the temple: 'you are forever opposing the Holy Spirit, just as your ancestors used to do' (7:51). It is too simple to see this only in terms of a division between Jewish Christians and other Jews, because it also reflects disagreement within the Jewish-Christian community. An idealised picture of agreement in the Early Church is in danger of misrepresenting Judaism simply as the opposition.

Into the future

Christopher Rowland rightly points out that both for Jews and for Christians, 'when we speak of the future hope we are dealing with something integral to faith.' The hope of the final vindication of God's people has its roots in the covenant relationship (2 Sam. 7:8f), and the belief in the coming of a new age of justice and peace is firmly established in the Jewish Scriptures (Isa. 11; Ezek. 40ff; Zech. 8:20ff; 9–14).[23]

AMEN. COME, LORD JESUS

It is sometimes said that whereas first century Judaism was looking forward to God's liberation of the land of Israel, the early Christian community looked back to an act of salvation for the world, centred not on Jerusalem but in Christ. However, it should also be recognised that there is something of 'present salvation' in the thought of a Greek-speaking Jew like the philosopher Philo, who can write: 'Belief in God, life-long joy, the perpetual vision of the Existent – what can anyone conceive more profitable or more august than these' (*Praem. Poen.* 27); and there is an element of 'present justification' in the faith of the Qumran community: 'From the source of his righteousness is my justification, and from his marvellous mysteries is the light in my heart.'[24] It should also be noted that, within the New Testament, the letter of James understands divine deliverance almost entirely in terms of the future (Jas. 1:1–12; 5:7–11).

In the dynamic process of the fulfilment of the promise, there will always be past, present and future liberation. Paul can say that 'salvation has come' (Rom. 11:11), that the cross is the power of God 'to us who are being saved' (1 Cor. 1:18), and that 'salvation is nearer to us now than when we became believers' (Rom. 13:11).

The proclamation of the nearness of future salvation and final vindication is found in the earliest and in the latest New Testament writings: for example, in 1 Thessalonians: 'we who are alive, who are left until the coming of the Lord, will by no means precede those who have died' (1 Thess.

29

4:15), and in Revelation, completed, perhaps, nearly half a century later: 'The one who testifies to these things says, "Surely I am coming soon." Amen. Come, Lord Jesus!' (Rev. 22:20).

In Revelation there is a remarkable interweaving of past, present and future tenses. In John's first vision the slaughtered Lamb takes the scroll from the one on the throne (Rev. 5:7) and the whole creation joins the angelic worship, 'singing, "To the one seated on the throne and to the Lamb be blessing and honour and glory and might forever and ever!" And the four living creatures said, "Amen!" And the elders fell down and worshipped' (5:13f). This is a vision of the past: the scroll, which the Lamb has not yet opened, contains God's whole will for his world and is most probably to be identified with the Hebrew Scriptures. The Lamb will be able to open the scroll because he is its subject and he will accomplish God's purpose. This vision is also of the present: it is the slaughtered Lamb who takes the scroll, for the crucified Christ is risen, and as he takes it the heavenly choir breaks into 'a new song' (5:9). And this first vision is also of the future: 'every creature' joins together in worship in final response to all that God has accomplished in Christ (5:13f). But in the future lies also John's eating of the scroll (10:8–10) and the role of the Lamb's followers, who by their witness will share his victory and his bringing the world to repentance and to worship. This indeed is a single vision of the God 'who is and who was and who is to come' (1:4, 8; cf. 4:8).

The exotic imagery of John's apocalyptic visions may evoke some sympathy with those Jewish rabbis who in the Mishnah warn the mystic who wants to look into what is above and below, what has been and what will be: 'it were better for him if he had not come into the world' (Hagigah 2:1). Perhaps it is time to return to Paul's movement from the past, for the present and into the future, focusing on his use of the title 'Israel' for God's people.

ALL ISRAEL WILL BE SAVED

Remembering the past, Paul uses the term 'Israelite' for himself (Rom. 11:1; 2 Cor. 11:22) and for his kindred (Rom.

9:4; 2 Cor. 11:22), and most frequently uses 'Israel' histori-cally[25] for the people to whom God gave the law and made his promises. Paul can still refer to this 'Israel' as God's people (Rom. 11:1f), identifying himself with them as 'my own people' (Rom. 9:3), and making the distinction between 'we Jews' (Rom. 3:9) and 'you Gentiles' (Rom. 11:13).

Considering the present, Paul also identifies himself with those called to belong to Jesus Christ, speaking of 'us whom he has called, not from the Jews only but also from the Gentiles' (Rom. 9:24; cf. 8:23), and going on to apply Hosea's prophecy of the restoration of Israel (Hos. 1:10) to the inclusion of Gentiles with Jews in the people of God: 'Those who were not my people I will call "my people"' (Rom. 9:25).[26] It is almost certain, given that he is summa-rising the main thrust of his letter, that Paul's reference in Galatians to 'the Israel of God' (Gal. 6:16) is not to historic Israel (either as a whole or as a remnant) but is instead to the Church – that is, to those Jews and Gentiles who are 'one in Christ Jesus' (Gal. 3:28).

Looking to the future, Paul's conviction is that 'all Israel will be saved' (Rom. 11:26). There is, of course, a significant debate about the meaning of 'all Israel' here. There are those who interpret the phrase as referring to the Jews (variously to all, to most, or to some) who are to be included with 'the full number of the Gentiles' (Rom. 11:25). Others, perhaps more persuasively, interpret 'all Israel' to mean the whole people of God, regardless of race – in other words, all those to whom God may be merciful (Rom. 11:32). Paul, seeking to persuade Gentile Christians that God has not rejected 'past Israel' and to persuade Jewish Christians that God does not limit 'present Israel' to the boundaries of the law, is certain only that God will fulfil his promise and accomplish his purpose. This leaves open some of the questions about 'future Israel' and the final identity of the people of God. Some years later and in another context the same openness is to be found in the first letter of John: 'Beloved, we are God's children now; what we will be has not yet been revealed. What we do know is this: when he is revealed, we shall be like him, for we shall see him as he is' (1 John 3:2).

It is not surprising that there continues to be lively debate about the meaning of 'Israel', particularly in Galatians 6:16 and in Romans 11:26. When Paul himself can say, with a sharpness which is blunted in many translations, 'they are not all Israel, which are of Israel' (Rom. 9:6 AV), then we must recognise that he is using the one name to hold together continuity and change, the old and the new. He finds the focal point of this dynamic process in Christ, the Messiah who is the offspring of Abraham (Gal. 3:16), but he argues that from the time of Abraham himself (Rom. 9:6ff) it has always been the case that 'they are not all Israel, which are of Israel,' and that change and continuity, the new and the old, belong intimately together.

Yesterday and today and forever

THE DYNAMIC OF SCRIPTURE

> Now I would remind you, brothers and sisters, of the good news that I proclaimed to you, which you in turn received, in which also you stand, through which also you are being saved, if you hold firmly to the message that I proclaimed to you – unless you have come to believe in vain (1 Cor. 15:1f).

Paul handed on to the Corinthians the Gospel which he himself had received: 'that Christ died for our sins in accordance with the scriptures, and that he was buried, and that he was raised on the third day in accordance with the scriptures' (1 Cor. 15:3f). This tradition holds together the story of Israel in *the Scriptures*, the person and work of *Christ*, who died and was raised, and the life of Paul's congregation: he died for *our sins*.

This pattern is fundamental to the New Testament and is well illustrated by Hebrews, which similarly brings together the Scriptures, Christ, and the group it addresses. Aware that not to move forwards is to move backwards (Heb. 6:1–6), the writer wishes his Jewish Christian readers, some of whom have been neglecting the Christian assembly (10:25), finally to break with the seeming securities of

Jewish liturgy (13:9–14), and to regain their confidence in worship and life in Christ (13:15f). It may be that it was the events of the Jewish revolt of AD 66–70, culminating in the destruction of the temple by the Romans, that were persuading this group that they were, after all, Jews. But the author sees this as a time to move forwards, 'outside the camp' (Heb. 13:13), and not to move backwards by falling away (6:4–6; 10:26–31). To be bereft of priest and sacrifice was to be exposed as an atheist,[27] and so the author quotes Psalm 110:4, identifying 'a priest forever' as Jesus (Heb. 5:6; 7:17, 21), and developing a tradition that has already seen Psalm 110:1 as God's words to Christ: 'Sit at my right.'[28] The group need not fear dispossession because 'we have a great high priest' (Heb. 4:1; 8:1; 10:21) and 'we have an altar' (13:10). Moving forward from the group's belief that Jesus is at God's right hand, the author invites them to see him as the true priest ministering in the 'true tent'. We have seen that he finds this non-Levitical priesthood in the Jewish Scriptures, and he also finds there the heavenly sanctuary, in God's words to Moses about the earthly one: 'See that you make everything according to the pattern that was shown you on the mountain' (Exod. 25:40, quoted in Heb. 8:5). In the Scriptures he also finds another sacrifice, in Psalm 40:6–8 (quoted in Heb. 10:5–7). The psalmist makes it clear that God does not desire 'burnt offerings and sin offerings' although, as Hebrews points out provocatively, 'these are offered according to the law' (Heb. 10:8). Instead, the psalmist's offering is willing obedience to the will of God: 'I have come to do your will, O God (in the scroll of the book it is written of me).' Jesus' accomplishment of God's will is both the true sacrifice which the psalmist envisaged and the fulfilment of Jeremiah's prophecy of a new covenant, because what was written in the book is now realised in practice. It is both to the sacrifice and to the covenant that the author refers when he adds: 'He abolishes the first in order to establish the second' (Heb. 10:9). This is certainly the time to move forward.

By such a provocative juxtaposition of a psalm questioning sacrifice and the law demanding it, the letter to the Hebrews picks up the dynamic of the Scriptures, finding

33

them to point outside themselves to the sacrifice of Christ. By returning to the Scriptures he finds in them another priesthood and another sanctuary, which will enable his readers to see that in Christ they have all that they need to move forward into the future. The author undoubtedly shares with those gathered to hear his words the faith that 'Jesus Christ is the same yesterday and today and forever' (Heb. 13:8); and yet to realise this they must now see him as they have not previously seen him, as 'a great high priest' who can lead them from the security of 'the camp' towards 'the city that is to come' (13:13f).

READING THE BIBLE

In George Gershwin's *Porgy and Bess*, Sporting Life sings to the picnicking crowd of poor blacks:

> It ain't necessarily so,
> It ain't necessarily so,
> De t'ings dat yo' li'ble
> To read in de Bible,
> It ain't necessarily so.[29]

Paul 'handed on' what Jesus did and said on the night he was 'handed over' (1 Cor. 11:23). The repetition of the word is a salutary reminder that we can betray as well as pass on our inheritance. It is doubtless the ways in which some have used the Bible that have led others to look elsewhere for freedom and life. It is perhaps a sense that the Scriptures are amenable to the Church that has encouraged some to ignore them and others to be endlessly fascinated with conspiracy theories about ancient scrolls and supposed secrets of apocryphal gospels. But, as Sporting Life might have found in the Bible itself, 'it ain't necessarily so.' It is open to anyone who wishes to study the Scriptures to find that things are not always what they seem. For example, we have seen that what is presented as old law or teaching sometimes represents new practice or thinking, and that what may seem at first to be radically different may sometimes be drawing on what is most conservative within the tradition.

This study suggests that we may find our own particular

habits of mind and ways of being represented among the many voices of the Scriptures, and it also argues that we will find much more. The authority of the Scriptures is not only the authority of a community whose response to God produced these texts and gradually determined their canonical status. It is also an authority over that community, which recognised these Scriptures for what they were and received them as a gift from God. And so we find that the canon of Scripture will not allow us to remember only what we find congenial and to ignore what we find perplexing. There is an integrity about the Bible, which reinterprets but does not silence its past, presenting to us both the old and the new covenants. There is a generosity about it, as it holds together for us different answers to these questions of continuity and change. As we read the Scriptures they involve us in their tension between the old and the new, drawing us into their conversation of voices. They encourage us to move forwards together in the dynamic process of realising the promise of the God of Israel, who is the God of Jesus, and who is our God: 'I will take you as my people, and I will be your God.'

Notes to Chapter 1

1 'Declaration of Assent' from Canon C15 of *The Canons of the Church of England* (London, Church House Publishing, 5th edn, 1993), p. 96.
2 The two examples are used by Peter R. Ackroyd, *Studies in the Religious Tradition of the Old Testament* (London, SCM, 1987), p. 247.
3 See the discussion of these passages in Michael Fishbane, *Biblical Interpretation in Ancient Israel* (Oxford, Clarendon Press, 1985), pp. 309–12. Other material in the present chapter draws on his analysis of 'inner-biblical exegesis'.
4 *Aspects of Aristocracy* (Newhaven and London, Yale University Press, 1994), pp. 33f.
5 See Ronald Williamson, *Jews in the Hellenistic World: Philo of Alexandria* (Cambridge, CUP, 1989), pp. 144–200. On the allegory in Galatians see, e.g., J. D. G. Dunn, *The Theology of Paul's Letter to the Galatians* (Cambridge, CUP, 1993), pp. 95–8.
6 An argument used both by Philo, e.g. *Spec. Leg.* 1:27, and by the rabbis, e.g. *Sanhedrin* 107b.

7 W. D. Davies, *Torah in the Messianic Age and/or the Age to Come* (Philadelphia, Society of Biblical Literature, 1952), p. 48.

8 *The Damascus Document* 6:19, trans. Geza Vermes, *The Dead Sea Scrolls in English* (London, Penguin, 4th edn, 1995), p. 102; cf. 8:21 (Vermes, p. 104).

9 *The Damascus Document* 16:1f (Vermes, p. 106).

10 Mark 12:31; cf. Luke 10:27; *Gen. Rab.* 24:7; *Sifra* 89b.

11 In Jas. 2:8, as in 1 Cor. 15:3f, 'according to the scripture' should be understood as 'in accordance with the scripture'. By the keeping of the royal law (i.e. the whole law of God) the scripture is fulfilled: 'you shall love your neighbour as yourself' (Lev. 19:18).

12 For the rabbinic attitude see, e.g., *Sifre Num.* 134; *P. Taanith* 65b.

13 *Jesus and Judaism* (London, SCM, 1985), p. 268.

14 See Ulrich Luz, *The Theology of the Gospel of Matthew* (Cambridge, CUP, 1995), pp. 11–15; E. P. Sanders, *The Historical Figure of Jesus* (London, Penguin, 1993), pp. 210–12;

15 *Jesus and Judaism*, op. cit., pp. 3–22.

16 Ibid., pp. 256–60.

17 See Simon J. De Vries, *From Old Revelation to New* (Grand Rapids, Eerdmans, 1995), p. 165.

18 See Fishbane, *Biblical Interpretation in Ancient Israel*, pp. 332–4.

19 Matt. 26:28; Mark 14:24; Luke 22:20.

20 Philo discusses such views in *Migr. Abr.* 89–93; cf. also *Sib. Or.* 4:24–30.

21 See Philip Francis Esler, *Community and Gospel in Luke-Acts* (Cambridge, CUP, 1987), pp. 154–61.

22 John Dominic Crossan, *The Historical Jesus: The Life of a Mediterranean Peasant* (Edinburgh, T. & T. Clark, 1993), p. 355.

23 *Christian Origins* (London, SPCK, 1985), p. 87.

24 *The Community Rule* 11:5 (Vermes, p. 87). See further N. T. Wright, *The New Testament and the People of God* (London, SPCK, 1992), pp. 334–8. One weakness of this excellent study of the relationship between *the story of Israel* and *the story of Jesus* is that it marginalises Philo within Judaism and excludes consideration of the letter of James from Christianity.

25 Rom. 9:27, 31; 10:19, 21; 11:2, 7, 25; 1 Cor. 10:18; 2 Cor. 3:7, 13; Phil. 3:5.

26 See also the use of Deut. 32:43 in Rom. 15:10 and of Lev. 26:11f and Ezek. 37:27 in 2 Cor. 6:16.

27 See, e.g., *The Martyrdom of Polycarp* 9; Justin Martyr, *1 Apology* 5f.

28 Used in Hebrews at 1:3, 13; 8:1; 10:12. See also Matt. 22:44; Mark 12:36; Luke 20:42; Acts 2:34; 1 Cor. 15:25. The use in Hebrews both of Ps. 110 and of Ps: 8 (Heb. 2:6ff) may also depend upon a connection already made in the Christian tradition; cf. 1 Cor. 15:25–27; Eph. 1:20–23; 1 Pet. 3:22.

29 Lyrics by Du Bose Heyward, first performed in 1935.

2 Performance and Presence: The Quest for Reality in Liturgical Worship

David Stancliffe

Introduction

In an era when there is a radical sense of discontinuity between the past and the present; when the figure of Jesus of Nazareth seems ever more distant from the experience of contemporary Christians; and when present experience of a lively faith appears to owe little to the sense of continuity in the tradition 'to which the historic formularies of the Church of England bear witness', we have an urgent task in holding past, present and future together. Is the past all past? And is our access to the past solely an exercise of memory? Is God's future so unfathomable that we are not only unmoved by the thought of heaven and hell, but feel unable to do more than close our eyes to it, burrowing under the bedclothes of present experience? Where is reality in our knowledge of God's presence?

These are questions I wish to address from the perspective of what holds past, present and future together in the experience of the Church at worship – the liturgy.

Liturgical reconstructions

Our contemporary experience of getting to grips with what is going on in the liturgy is paralleled by the kind of discussions going on in the world of early music:

> Indifference to the past is one of the failings of our time. Some discern a 'deliberate neglect of history, a trashing of works which

37

do not fit contemporary fads and prejudices, with the loss of biblical and poetic memory . . .'[1] Perhaps we may say that 'liturgical reconstructions' are among the most valuable contributions that early-music performance can make to the civilisation in which we live. I have no commitment to the dissemination of Christian belief, but I do have a commitment to the preservation of 'biblical and poetic memory' in an age when 'our inner spaces are [being] jammed with raucous trivia.'[2] The liturgy is a lexicon of such memories, and one that has not yet been entirely overwritten with 'theory': there are few books at present with titles like *Gender and Desire in the Sarum Ordinal* or *Writing the Unwriteable: the Poetics of the Offertory Trope.*

So wrote Christopher Page, director of Gothic Voices, in the *Early Music Review* for March 1996, where there was an interesting exchange between a number of performers and editors of early music on the validity and worthwhileness of 'liturgical reconstructions', as they have come to be known in the early music industry. In the search for authenticity, for allowing the listener access to virtual reality in early music, there has been a growing tendency to set works like the Monteverdi *Vespers* in a 'churchy' frame. For a long time the value of creating the right ambience for live performances of such works has been recognised: anyone who has conducted a performance of one of the Bach Passions in a church with some of the qualities of the Thomaskirche in Leipzig on Passion Sunday, for example, recognises that. In his Ceremony of Carols, Benjamin Britten frames his carol settings with a Gregorian antiphon to give them a prehistory and a harmonic context. But the musicians in dialogue in the *Early Music Review* are not just concerned with creating a romantic atmosphere: they are trying to discover and deliver to us reality.

What makes for reality in the performance of works like Monteverdi's *Vespers of the Blessed Virgin Mary* of 1610? We do not even know that this work was written primarily for performance: the psalm settings look astonishingly like a virtuoso display of enormously different techniques in handling a Gregorian *cantus firmus*. What we have in the volume which Monteverdi published are not only the psalms, hymn and two Magnificats for Vespers, but also a Mass and a number of Motets. It is like a list of ingredients, without the recipe. There is none of the necessary plainchant, for example, and supplying the right pieces is quite an art; was the work, dedicated to the Pope and probably published in order to try and get a post in Rome, written with San Marco in Venice in mind, or does it reflect the Gonzaga chapel at Mantua, in neither of which was the Roman rite used strictly? And to make it sound and feel like Vespers, what do you need? A church of the right size and shape? A priest or two? Clouds of incense? Will such reconstructions ever be wholly convincing? Are not the attempts to reproduce every detail painstakingly bound to stifle the freshness of a genuinely authentic performance now? When Heinrich Schutz published his *Historia der Geburt Jesus Christi* in 1664 he published the narrative, the recitative, rather than the entrancing *intermedii* or concerted numbers that seem such gems to us but which, he said, you could replace with your own if you liked: 'use my structure, but assemble your own ingredients if you know what you are doing' recognises that repeated performances will change, and points us beyond the carefully constructed liturgical reconstructions of today to something more like the layered experience of a living worship tradition, where the order of the Book of Common Prayer is used alongside the hymnody of Charles Wesley with a contemporary sermon and pattern of intercession.

The exchange in the *Early Music Review* centred on the difference between music performed as the self-contained art-form that we have been taught to expect today and music as a continuing and vital part of a living liturgical celebration, where it functions to add to the solemnity of the rite and lets it breathe. While it will always help if musicians understand something of the liturgy whose music they are performing, most of the corespondents recognised that no performance of the music divorced from its genuine context in worship is likely to be more than a 'concert performance', as it would be called if we were talking about an unstaged opera.

What was particularly interesting about the exchange,

however, was that there emerged among that group of musicians – few of whom clearly are practising worshippers – a sense of longing to enter the mind-set of a previous age of which the surviving liturgical music was only one fragment. What about the priest's liturgy – all of it – including all that was said under the breath? And the people's too, with all those mumbled Hail Marys and Paternosters, and their Amens? And what about the buildings in which the liturgy was celebrated? What was the actual experience of those worshippers, and can we understand the music written for the liturgies they celebrated better by trying to enter that reality?

Live performance and the composer's score

All these nuances pale into insignificance, however, beside the major question which any musical performance poses: what is the relationship between the composer's score and the interpreter – the performer? Unlike the painter, who completes his canvas which then hangs there for anyone to see and react to how they will (and this depends on their cultural conditioning, their imaginative skills and their understanding of the language of the artist), the composer writes a score and publishes it; he then waits for other musicians – be they individuals, a chamber group or even an orchestra with its conductor – to realise the score in a performance. The performance – partly because so much music is readily available on disc and at the touch of a button – is only one stage in the music being brought alive to the hearer. How far is this intermediate stage of interpretive performance a potentially hazardous dislocation in realising the composer's intentions, or how far is it a genuine opportunity for the performer's creative engagement in the process, without which it would never capture our interest and deliver actual music?

There is a parallel analogy: the recipe for a classic dish – say *coq au vin* – has been the same for 100 or 200 years, or more. But is it the same dish, the same taste, the same experience? It is made in the same way, by cooks in a succession, who have learnt their skills from one another in a community of interest. They have the same intention: to make that classic French dish. But it will taste different each time, depending on the quality of the wine (is it best burgundy?), or the salt pork and the bird. And do we rear cocks as they did 100 years ago? Or do we make our burgundy the same? The answer may be 'no', but it will not be an offence against the Trade Descriptions Act if we follow our classic recipe with the best ingredients we can find and intend to produce *coq au vin*, whereas it would certainly be if we just boiled a chicken and heated it in a ready-made, commercially produced, packet sauce – whose chief ingredient was monosodium glutamate! As two respected French chefs observe in the contemporary war against novel creations in the kitchen, 'a great dish is a testament to simplicity and harmony of flavours; [it] draws from sources and the inspiration of our collective memory.'[3]

The question is not just one about continuity: it is also about the transferability of identity between the creator and the realiser; and between the realiser and the recipient. The recipients trust that what they will hear (or eat) is what the composer (or chef) meant them to hear (or taste). The difficulty is posed particularly sharply in the case of early music, when – for the most part – even the 'score' is often a modern invention, created maybe from a series of part-books, and with no indication from the composer about which voices or instruments are to be used, and often with little indication of the pitch or dynamic at which the piece is to be performed. So much depends on the performers' knowledge of the musical conventions: I remember as a student singing through material from the Eton Choirbook and finding that soaringly ecstatic music dreary in the extreme, simply because we did not understand anything about the performing conventions. We were misled by the notation, and it turned out that we were singing it at less than half speed.

The early musicians' commitment to interpreting this one part of the Western tradition is very illuminating. Their concern is expressed from the specialised, post-Christian viewpoint of professional musicians and is not just about understanding a set of musical conventions; it embraces an

41

attempt to grasp the identity of a cultural, not just a lit- urgical, context which has undergone a series of radical discontinuities over the past 450 years in particular.

Performing the liturgy

But their concern could be ours. The proper performance of the liturgy offers a parallel which, if not exact in every detail, offers us some major similarities. There is a basic 'score', the saving acts of God in Jesus Christ, there is the Christian community's repeated rehearsal of this score in its offering of worship – a 'performance tradition' which has an unbroken history, however radical some of the cultural and theological disjunctions may appear; and there is the effect of this in the transformed lives of countless Christians over the centuries. Week by week in the celebration of the Eucharist on Sundays, year by year in the celebration of the two cycles which celebrate incarnation and redemption around the birth and the death and resurrection of Jesus respectively, and lifetime by lifetime as new Christians enter this chain of celebration in baptism and so continue to reinvigorate, hand on and live out the embodied life of Christ in a way that both creates it afresh in each age and culture, and sustains its members through achievement and disaster, this pattern is repeated. We too have a series of performing conventions, and one of the skills which we ought to be able to assume in our clergy is competence if not in performing, then at least in 'performance practice'. This performance – as the celebration of the liturgy is – is focused in the Eucharist, which is the activity which defines the Church as Church, the continuously remade assembly of those called by God to live 'in Christ' as a sign of his coming Kingdom.

But is it the same Eucharist, the same music? Is Christ present to us in the same way as he was to the apostles when they met behind locked doors? Is there a thread which binds Christian experience together over so many centuries, in spite of differences of culture and language, and huge shifts in metaphysical understanding? Is there a reality about the presence of Christ among his people as they offer themselves in union with him to the Father in worship which remains constant, however, wherever, whenever it is expressed? Is the score capable of performance in such different contexts and with such different players and instruments that the music remains recognisably the same? What was the sense of union with God which the Christians of previous generations experienced and then sought, consciously or not, to encapsulate or frame in the acts of liturgical worship which they celebrated? And most particularly, what was the emerging liturgy's relationship with the experience of the first disciples? Above all, does the worshipping tradition in which we stand offer us an experience which is continuous with theirs?

There are many Christians today for whom questions like this are, at best, irrelevant. We cannot know how our forbears felt; and what matters to us is *our* experience, *now*. Understanding the past, how worship came to have the form and content that it did, answers no more than the antiquarian questions, and cannot help us to make that spontaneous offering of ourselves in worship to the living God today.

I cannot be content with this approach, any more than I can be content with the view that if Bach had had a Steinway grand and a full Wagnerian orchestra of twentieth century instruments, he would not have bothered with the thin-toned fiddles and harpsichords he actually wrote for. He might well have written splendidly for modern instruments, but he would not have written what he did, as he did. As far as the liturgy is concerned, I am clear that it is in the continuing and unbroken experience of liturgical worship that the whole raft of our relationship with the one who is both the Jesus of history, the living Lord of the Church and the cosmic Christ who is to come is sustained. Of course, there is more to the liturgy than that: it is the liturgy that carries doctrine. I believe firmly with Prosper of Aquitaine that *legem credendi lex statuat supplicandi* and recognise that this is particularly true of the Church of England, where our formularies are rooted in the Book of Common Prayer, the Thirty-Nine Articles and the

Ordering of Bishops, Priests and Deacons. Nor should we be side-tracked into believing that this raft is engined over-whelmingly by the past. The exciting pull for Christians is the gift of the future. We are those whose destiny is hidden with Christ, says the First Letter of John: 'My friends, it does not yet appear what we shall be, but we know that when he appears we shall be like him, for we shall see him as he is' (1 John 3:2).

While too much liturgical archaeology may well divert our attention from the experience of the present, too much attention to the present may leave us without any sense of our belonging with our fellow Christians over the centuries as well as without any sense of the direction in which God may be taking us. 'The essential nature of the future lies in the unpredictable new thing that is hidden in the womb of the past.'[4]

Looking for presence

What then *is* the relationship between the Last Supper, the Church's celebration of the Eucharist today, and our destiny? Or – to take a more layered approach – between the feeding of the people of Israel in the wilderness with manna, the feeding of the five thousand by Jesus, the Last Supper, the death of Jesus Christ on the cross, the breaking of the bread at the supper at Emmaus, the celebratory meal described by St Paul in 1 Corinthians, the Eucharist described in the Apostolic Tradition of Hippolytus, the rite of Sarum, the Eucharist from the *Alternative Service Book 1980* celebrated in the parish churches of England today and the heavenly banquet, that eloquent image of God's coming Kingdom? Are our liturgical acts in the Church today no more than 'liturgical reconstructions' – vivid, one-off re-enactments which enable us to enter creatively and imaginatively into an event or events in the life of Christ in such a way that we can feel their power? Or is there a continuity and a reality to our liturgy? How is Christ really present to us in the liturgy? And what are we becoming, by taking a regular part in the celebration?

This question of Christ's presence in the liturgy has all

too often in the past been narrowly focused on theories of consecration, and been part of the traditional Catholic/Reformed battleground, fuelled by assuming a Thomist metaphysical system on the one hand, or a Lutheran mis-reading of the Canon Missae on the other. But historically, the question of presence is more complex and less well defined. Earlier and less mechanistic or transactional lan-guage spoke of Christians at the Eucharist participating in 'making the offering', rather than simply being present 'to receive communion'. In later practice, object has replaced activity as the focus of the rite: the sense of engagement in the movement of Christ's self-offering to the Father becomes replaced by the moment of receiving the host, with the consequent difficulties of deciding precisely how and when the bread became the body, which led to an elaborate theology of sacrificial priesthood and a 'moment' theology of consecration, both concepts unfamiliar to the earliest levels of the tradition. In an interesting essay on the Windsor Statement and the Eucharistic Prayer,[5] Thomas Talley explores the relationship between Oblation and Con-secration in the recent post-Conciliar Eucharistic prayers in both the Roman and Anglican traditions, and consecration of the gifts and the institution narrative might have been disentangled by giving some attention to the process of development through which the prayer itself has gone, and then allowing the theology to flow from it, the theological preconceptions of the participants in the ARCIC conver-sations set the agenda, rather than letting the Eucharist itself as we have prayed it and experienced it teach us how to realise Christ's presence.

Christ is present in the assembly of the baptised, in the proclamation of the Gospel – the Word made flesh, in the prayer to the Father that his will be done, in joining ourselves to the sacrifice of Christ, in the offering of praise and thanksgiving, in the breaking of the bread, in the sharing of the gifts that we may be made one, in the renewed commitment to live out Christ's life for the sake of his people, in the proclamation in our common life of his coming Kingdom – yes, and all this focused in the one bread of heaven, formed of the fruit of the earth by human hands, and broken that we might have life, unity and peace. But even if the bread is where the focus lies, the bread too contains within its creation, significance and use a whole process of change and transformation.

With this complex history of process and focus in the search for the reality of Christ's presence, I suggest that there might be three aspects of the performance of the liturgy in the Church which we might explore under the headings of memory, presence and encounter.

Memory, presence and encounter

In a recent and interesting book, *Memory and Salvation*,[6] Charles Elliott explores the ways in which our memories form us, and indeed to a large extent govern our reaction to our entire experience. Elliott is primarily concerned with how we, as a people and a Church, as well as individuals, can be set free from our memories by Christ. In the brief theological reflections at the end of his work, Elliott suggests that the Church's (corrected) memories of Jesus can be set alongside our own conscious and unconscious memories as a source of transformation: Jesus has both a remembered past and a future destiny, and this may set us free. Leaving aside the lack of clarity about how these memories are to be laid alongside one another in a creative way, the question which he raises but does not explore is where the 'memory' of Christ becomes in any sense real:

> what matters is not, in fact, the facticity of the memories we encounter in the [biblical] text, but what we do with them. Like Joan Riviere's patient, we find that what matters is 'what we do with them inside ourselves' – for it is out of that salvation can come. In a word, we are back to hermeneutics. Interpretation is, it seems, all.[7]

Can we be saved by interpretation? The hermeneutic task is made difficult in principle for two reasons which mirror one another: there is the general cultural relativity which is part of current Western experience and delivers to us an immense sense of almost solipsistic individualism; and there is the parallel collapse of any agreed metaphysical

framework, which makes it difficult for us to give ontological reality to events and experiences beyond the limits
of our own knowledge and perception, particularly if we
are conceiving ourselves as substantially our memories.
However, Elliott hints that the process has something to do
with worship:

> The community of memory does not, then, exist as it were for its
> own benefit, but for the worship of God. And it is in that
> worship, with its memory-centred processes of reading the Scrip-
> tures, celebrating the sacraments and praising God for what he
> has shown himself to be and for what he has done in individual
> and collective histories, that the atoning work of Christ is
> appropriated ... The more the community is enabled to
> 'remember this', the more the work of Christ is appropriated –
> and the more the Church can then become an agent of the
> Kingdom of God.[8]

Elliott has grasped the importance of the worshipping tradition of the Church as the prime holder of memory, but his
model of a community of memory speaks to me more
clearly of an abstract, intellectual temple of thought-forms,
rather than the crucible of reality. I suspect that he realises
this, because he grasps at the reality of memory primarily in
terms of re-presentation:

> The memory is not just a cognitive process, highly intellectual-
> ised. It is acted memory, re-membering, re-presentation. This is
> most obviously the case with the sacraments, but it is also incar-
> nated in buildings, ornaments, art, songs, movement and dance,
> vestment and attire. The Church is a theatre of memory, with its
> scripts, its scenery, its proscenium and its music. The fact that the
> production is often lacklustre or half-hearted or unimaginative is
> hardly relevant to the point.[9]

The principal reason why the ever-repeated liturgy has
such an inescapable place in the life of the Church is
because it holds, focuses and transmits what Elliott calls
memory. But is that a sufficient description? It is true that
worship tells the story of the dealings of God with his
people: there are the biblical readings, and the psalms,
hymns and songs which tell it explicitly.

But the claim of the Church has always been that we do not just hear again what God once did, we celebrate his continuing activity in our lives. The sacraments do not only express something of the nature of God and our relationship with him, they also make something happen in the here and now to establish that relationship as reality, not merely as a mental construct. Baptism is not principally a dramatic celebration of our decision to die to our past by copying Christ's descent into the tomb and his being raised from death to life by the Father; baptism is the Church's celebration – Christ's action in his body – of what God has done for us in raising Christ from the dead. Baptism has an *epicletic*, a 'calling into being', as well as an *anamnetic* or 'remembering' dimension, and while *anamnesis* has the force of drawing the past up into the present, rather than casting our minds back into the past, it is in its activity of *epiclesis* that the Church claims the promise that the Spirit will be poured out, that God will act to fulfil the promise of his presence. Similarly, the celebration of the Eucharist in obedience to the Lord's command 'do this in remembrance of me' is not merely a dramatised *aide-mémoire* of the Last Supper, a vivid and dramatic way of casting our minds back to that Upper Room; it is a celebration of the one sacrifice of Christ, made present and lively – as the Book of Common Prayer puts it – in our midst. For though the one oblation of himself once offered is the full, perfect and sufficient sacrifice, oblation and satisfaction for the sins of the whole world, yet Christ's sacrifice is eternally present before God and has as its object, not death, but life. R. C. Moberly makes this point with clarity:

> The culminating point of the sacrifice was not in the shedding of the blood, but in the presentation before God, in the holy place, of the blood that had been shed; of the life, that is, which had passed through death, and had been consecrated to God by dying. It is not the death itself which is acceptable to the God of life: but the vital self-identification with the holiness of God, the perfect self-dedication and self-surrender which is represented.[10]

This 'vital self-identification' is the process we can see being recognised, and then celebrated in the biblical material:

why did Jesus fast 40 days in the wilderness, where he fed on the word of God among the stones? What has this to do with the 40 years the people of Israel wandered in the wilderness, supposedly feeding on the manna from heaven, but – we know – actually feeding on the word of God which Moses brought down from the mountain? How does this biblical technique affect the way in which we read the account of the journey of the disciples to Emmaus on the day of resurrection? We know that the stranger who walked with them spent a good deal of the time on the way explaining the way in which Jesus of Nazareth had fulfilled the Old Testament prophesies about the Messiah, the anointed one. This kind of christological completion of the law and the prophets may well have been responsible for the selection and arrangement of the material which we now know as the Gospels.[11] So when the author of Luke/Acts describes the worship of the infant Church as 'day by day, attending the temple together and breaking of bread in their homes', he was already articulating an established pattern where the Christ could be known in his Church as the living presence in the breaking of the bread, and also be the one who fulfilled history and 'redeemed Israel' (Luke 24:21).

What was real? First, that the Christ was revealed in the moment of the breaking of bread. This action – and it seems to have been the archetypal action of what became established as the Church's Eucharist – was the moment that became ritualised in what was to become the fraction at the Eucharist. It held together the breaking of the body on the cross, the moment of death, of sacrifice, when the life was released from the narrow prison of particularity, and the possibility for the many fragmented individuals who made up the Church, the body of Christ, being one, as they each received a small piece of the broken bread. In the mystery of Christ's death and disintegration lay the possibility of our completion and wholeness.

It is this very real activity, the breaking of bread which has been consecrated to be the body of Christ into small fragments, so that each may receive a piece and so be made one bread, one body, that constitutes the basic reality at the

49

heart of our worship. It is not words spoken, nor memories stirred, but something done between at least two of us which constitutes the focus of our life in Christ. It is in this doing, this change from a whole bread to broken fragments, when the fragmentariness of our transient individuality is given worth and dignity, and our self-absorbed lives are turned outwards and begin to find true fulfilment in relating to what is beyond us.

The sense that the liturgy is a corporate activity, not a solo performance with an audience, a dialogue between persons, not a monologue, a pattern of transformation which offers a glimpse of reality, not the delivery of a pre-determined dollop of some concocted substance, delivers us from the quest for substance into the longing for encounter, relationship and making real. In the account of the walk to Emmaus in Luke 24, there is already encounter, exposition, relationship, disclosure, reality, presence and fulfilment. The stages through which the disciples travel mirror the pattern of the liturgy, as they do the pattern of music-making. Encounter, relationship and fulfilment (or engagement, involvement and change) mark the stages not only of the forming of relationships, but in the process of turning the notes on the page of a score into harmony in the ears of the listener.

The liturgy offers encounter in the engagement between the person and his day-by-day agenda with the divine story, rehearsed in the liturgy of the sacraments, in the Church's year and in each individual's life-cycle; it offers relationship with the Godhead through absorption into the one prayer of the Son to the Father, into which we are drawn – in the sacramental life of the Church we grow into the clothes that have been draped around us in our baptism, becoming who we are called to be, Christlike, children of God; it offers fulfilment or transformation in the sense of unity, of completeness, which is only glimpsed but which is capable of fulfilment in a life lived fully at one with God's will. This is the point of the hymn:

> So, Lord, at length when sacraments shall cease,
> We may be one with all thy Church above,

One with thy saints in one unbroken peace,
One with thy saints in one unbounded love:
More blessed still, in peace and love to be
One with the Trinity in Unity.[12]

Transformation

The sense that Christ indwelt his Church powerfully was
certainly the view of Leo the Great in the fifth century. In a
sermon on the Ascension he said, 'all that was visible of the
Redeemer has passed over into the sacraments.' And by
the sacraments Leo meant the whole structure and pattern
of worship, including the liturgical year, the lectionary and
the ecclesial framework. But in an age which is deeply mis-
trustful of corporate ritual and is in danger of losing its
liturgical memory, these are questions which a Church
which is committed to exploring tradition and change
needs to address. We are, for example, brought up on
Shakespeare, and with the expectation that to be present at
a performance of a Shakespeare tragedy like *King Lear* will
transform us by putting us in touch with our interior well-
springs. In a fascinating study, Murray Cox and Alice
Theilgaard[13] show from their work with the highly disturbed how deeply the metaphors and images Shakespeare
uses connect with the interior landscapes of our fractured
memories. This is parallel to the expectations of the Athen-
ians of the fourth century BC that to witness a trilogy of
plays, for example by Aeschylus, was to undergo a profound religious experience with a cathartic or purging
effect. It did not matter if the material out of which the
dramas were woven was mythological in the sense that
the actual personages were idealised heroes of folk
memory: what was real was the conflict of duty and love,
the tragedy of inexorable fate, the way in which the
quarrels of the gods were played out in the innocent lives of
hapless mortals. The experience of the participants was
both sustaining and transforming, but where it touched
reality was in the realm of relationships, not in what was
ontologically effected. There was a sense in which the
effects were highly felt and emotionally charged at a con-

51

ceptual or intellectual level, while sitting very lightly to the reality of it all.

One interesting observation on the development of Greek theatre is that the more popular elements were gradually subsumed into the more intellectual. Greek drama began as the chants of the chorus on the *orchestra*, the circular dancing space on which they moved rhythmically as they sang. These hymns which expressed the people's fears and longings were the original liturgy. Only gradually did it become necessary to elaborate the dialogue between the actors on the stage above the dancing space which spelt out the context in which these ancient and heartfelt cries could be understood. And only then did attention begin to shift away from the hymns towards the interpersonal dramas – from common or social response to personal and individual feelings. This is parallel to the experience of the Dinka people in the Sudan: at the early stage of their Christian life, their creative energies went into the writing of hymns and songs, with dance and action, which expressed their feelings and reaction to the liberation brought by the Gospel; then at a later stage and more self-consciously they surrounded the basic sense of being delivered from their past by telling their story, and setting that against the biblical story of God's dealing with his captive people, and telling this by dialogue as well as by means of the epic bardic style.

Some of that has spilled over into how we feel about the practice of religion today: people feel that there is a myth of great significance embodied in the Christian story – an archetypal myth of transformation, even of the possibility of salvation, and they would dearly love to appropriate it for themselves. The formal worship of the Church at any rate allows them to eavesdrop on this world, where the thread of continuity which holds together the reality of their longing and the roots of memory is the celebration of the sacraments, of receiving the broken bread and the common cup.

But we too easily assume that the 'score' – what we have to perform in the church-making liturgical assembly – is fixed, that it was conceived and notated sometime 'before the creation of the world' and is a given. But this is to fly in the face of what we know about the nature of the Godhead. It assumes the fixity of the divine nature, and moreover the fixity – the substantive 'thingness' of God himself, as well as the fixity of human apprehension and human epistemological constructs, when all we know of the revelation of the divine nature is the essentially relational quality of God. It is in the life of the Godhead, the *koinonia*, or belonging together, which we glimpse in the interrelation of the Persons of the Holy Trinity, that we believe that God is visible. In this sense, the function of the liturgy is less like the establishment of good performance practice of the best texts of the scores that we can find, so that we can confidently claim authenticity by referring to some original sound, some close encounter with the Jesus of history's perfect self-offering to the Father. Instead it is more like the pursuit of a perfect harmony, once heard and every now and then glimpsed, or rather an echo caught in a pattern of notes, sounds, rhythms, phrases and sequences which offers to all the participants a part to play. This harmony has a subtle, ever-changing resonance like the music of the Aeolian harp; kaleidoscopically it continues to echo the divine harmony of the Godhead. This conscious pursuit of a perfect harmony in the Italian Renaissance was given expression not only in mathematical and musical constructs – in text, but also in context – for example, in Alberti's centrally planned churches in an attempt to create perfect sounds in perfect spaces.[14] This sprang from a desire not only to echo the harmony of heaven but to make those who came into contact with the experience perfect themselves. It was based on an organic model of transformation.

Real presence: George Herbert and the Passion

By way of a summary, let me return to the musical analogy, and set out how one artist with words manages to encapsulate a paradigm of memory, presence and relationship. First, let me pursue the musical analogy, and try and be more precise about just what happens in performance.

To make music, even of the most improvised kind, you need a score, or at least a set of conventions and a harmonic

53

framework within which to improvise. That is what the composer first conceives, then sets down in notation, and is what is delivered to the performers. The performers have their instruments prepared, and the parts in front of them; they work at the music, feeling their way into the composer's intentions by way of the hints in the score and the conventions they have learnt for performing music in this idiom until they have not only mastered the notes, but the style and sound-picture as well. Only then are they ready to perform the work, and how the performance is received depends not only on their skill and technique as performers of the notes on the page but also on the integrity of their interpretation. Does it have an internal consistency? Does it work with the grain of what the composer intended? These are questions which the music critic will articulate, but which every hearer will subconsciously be asking. There is a second sense about when the piece is ready to be performed, when rehearsal dulls into repetition. Rehearsal is hard work, and the Latin word for 'to rehearse' – *meditor* – gives more of the underlying sense of what is involved than the familiar English. To rehearse is to ponder, pattern yourself around and make three-dimensionally yours what is a two-dimensional score in notation.

As I have observed, music, unlike painting or sculpture, is a complex art where the originator – in this case the composer – has only part of the responsibility for delivering the finished article. It is in performance, in making actual in a particular place, time and context, that the work comes alive. Reading the score to yourself is a form of private purism which is hardly recognised by most as music! In this sense, what goes on between the writing of the score and hearing the music live is significant for understanding the relationship between the passion of Christ and the celebration of the Eucharist.

One of my friends is a violin maker, and from him I have learnt something of the risks involved in instrument making. Nowadays, it is relatively easy to get careful measured drawings of many of the world-famous instruments by Amati and Stradivarius and their lesser known contemporaries, a number of whose instruments have survived virtually unaltered, and the violin maker who is concerned to make accurate copies of historic instruments has plenty to go on. What I never appreciated before is the astonishingly fine balance between resonance and collapse in stringed instruments. Obviously, if the strings are slack, there can be no music: they must be tensioned to the point of collapse, which always tempts the maker to make just a bit thicker the belly of the instrument which sustains the bridge across which the strings are stretched. But the thicker the belly – or the sounding board, if it is a harpsi-chord – the less natural resonance there will be, and the duller the tone. In the history of the development of instruments, you can trace the demand for a richer, fuller tone leading inexorably to thicker strings, and the increased tension from thicker strings bowed by a heavier bow leading to a solider and so less naturally resonant belly, and to a continued spiral away from the natural point of balance. The maker's art is to judge the point of balance between soaring resonance and total collapse: too thick and there will be no resonance; too much slack in the string and you can get no tone.

In this poem 'Easter', George Herbert compared the passion of Christ to a stringed instrument:

> Awake my lute and struggle for thy part
> > With all thy art.
> The crosse taught all wood to resound his name
> > Who bore the same.
> His stretched sinews taught all strings, what key
> Is best to celebrate this most high day.

This courtier-turned-country-parson understood that the passion, the love of God, was a song, a music, that could only ring out from an instrument that was both thin and tightly strung. For there to be music, for the sound to be both beautiful and audible, that instrument had to risk col-lapse. Only the stretched sinews of Christ's body on the cross could let that music, that passion, be heard. To make music you need an instrument, and God's instrument was Christ.

Yet the poem is called not 'Passion', but 'Easter'. It looks beyond the struggle to produce the sound – the paraphernalia of tuning and technique – to the music, to the moment when the sound takes off, and harmony springs into being:

> Rise heart, thy Lord is risen. Sing his praise
> Without delayes
> Who takes thee by the hand that thou likewise
> With him mayest rise.

The music is more than the marriage of a well-tuned instrument and a good technique. If it is to lift its players, and so its hearers, some passion, some risk, some commitment, something stronger than death that many waters cannot quench is necessary. That life, that love can only be generated by the interaction between us, the players with our instruments, and the music, the composed score. Herbert is also interested in the spirit and not just in the mechanics, and so roots the experience in the life of the Trinity:

> O let thy blessed Spirit take a part
> and make up our defects with his sweet art.

There, in a performance made perfect in life and love, is the presence of God among us. George Herbert captures the essentially liturgical nature of Christ's death and resurrection – the lynch-pin of the faith – as something done, not said; a song sung rather than a doctrine thought about, re-expressed, restated in words. We look for the elusive presence of God in the way the liturgical tradition develops, and find we are not so much charting the development of the liturgical formularies – though that is a proper academic exercise – as responding to our changing experience of God. That response has a patterned form, a continuous history and the power to change. That change is not discontinuous, but primarily about the slow, seamless evolution of experience of God. In our tradition it is the liturgy which carries doctrine, and doctrine develops precisely because it is handed on, tested and forged in liturgical performance. The celebration of the liturgy shapes our experience of the divine, and forms our lives in the divine image. Past, present and future are made real and present in the Christ who comes among us and transforms the poverty of our humanity by the riches of his grace. But it is the action of grace, not the verbal explanations, which brings the real presence, which holds an ever-changing tradition in equipoise.

Notes to Chapter 2

1 Henry Porter, writing in *The Guardian* (1 Feb. 1996).
2 George Steiner, *No Passion Spent: Essays 1978–1996* (London, 1996).
3 Joel Robuchon and Alain Ducasse, *The Times* (23 May 1996).
4 Wolfhart Pannenberg, *Some Basic Questions in Theology*, Vol. 1 (London, SCM, 1970), p. 79.
5 Thomas J. Talley, *Worship Reforming Tradition* (Washington DC, The Pastoral Press, 1990), pp. 35–46.
6 Charles Elliott, *Memory and Salvation* (London, DLT, 1995).
7 Ibid., p. 252.
8 Ibid., p. 237.
9 Ibid., p. 221.
10 R. C. Moberly, *Ministerial Priesthood* (London, John Murray, 1897), p. 245.
11 M. D. Goulder, *Midrash and Lection in Matthew* (London, SPCK, 1974), and *The Evangelist's Calendar* (London, SPCK, 1978).
12 Col. W. H. Turton (*English Hymnal* 324).
13 *Mutative Metaphors in Psychotherapy – The Aeolian Mode* (London, Tavistock Publications, 1987).
14 See Rudolph Wittkower, *Architectural Principles in the Age of Humanism* (London, Alec Tiranti, 1962), pp. 27–30.

3 Seeing Life Whole: An Integrative Approach to the Christian Tradition

Perran Gay

> But be his
> My special thanks, whose even-balanced soul,
> From first youth tested up to extreme old age,
> Business could not make dull, or passion wild;
>
> Who saw life steadily, and saw it whole;
> The mellow glory of the Attic stage,
> Singer of sweet Colonus, and its child.[1]

Matthew Arnold chooses Sophocles as his mental and spiritual mentor because the Greek dramatist demonstrated for Arnold certain characteristics which he much admired, and which he perceived to be increasingly lacking in his contemporary society. In his essay in political and social criticism, *Culture and Anarchy*, Arnold frequently deplores the nineteenth century's obsession with organisation and machinery, machinery often seen as an end in itself, 'most absurdly disproportioned to the end which this machinery, if it is to do any good at all, is to serve'.[2] By contrast, Arnold advocates what he describes as culture, 'a study of perfection, a perfection which consists in becoming something rather than having something, in an inward condition of the mind and spirit, not in an outward set of circumstances.'[3] Part of that perfection consists for Arnold in the capacity that he attributes to Sophocles, an ability to see life steadily and see it whole. One of the marks of an integrated personality, the sort of person who is able to inspire and lead others, is the possession of an integrated vision, the understanding that life as a whole is greater than the sum of its parts.

Were we to substitute 'God' for 'life' and 'theology' for 'culture' in the above extracts, we would arrive at a definition of one of the chief aims of the theological enterprise, that is, to tell the whole truth about God. In the eighteenth of his lectures to catechumens, Cyril of Jerusalem gives a fivefold definition of the word 'Catholic' as applied to the Church. It is found *everywhere* and is not the special preserve of a particular race or group. It teaches the *whole* truth, all that is necessary for salvation. It makes holiness possible for *all* kinds of people, whatever their abilities or backgrounds. It is able to remedy and mend *all* the sicknesses and sins of our human condition. And it shows the fullest possible *variety* of human excellence and achievement.

Telling the whole truth, seeing life and God 'whole', is not facilitated by the contemporary fragmentation in theological thinking, due in part to the advent of increasing specialisation by scholars within particular theological disciplines, and indeed to the growth of the professional study of theology by those who are not necessarily believers. As a result, for instance, the conservative liturgist may well take the work of patristic scholars seriously but ignore entirely the work of New Testament critics. The biblical critic, on the other hand, may pursue her work without looking at some of the serious hermeneutical questions which may be raised by dogmaticians or ecclesiologists. Meanwhile, the doctrinal theologian may continue with his systematic or dogmatic approach to theology while ignoring the work of biblical scholars, except where the findings of the latter lend themselves to an easy synthesis with his own thinking. Christopher Evans comments with some feeling about this situation:

> The biblical theologian is not infrequently aware of the systematic theologian breathing down his neck in pursuit of a body of biblical material that shall be sufficiently coherent for the purposes of a systematic theology, and he is not insensitive to the exasperation he arouses when he fails to produce it. He knows

59

that he must appear awkward and unco-operative, constitution-
ally incapable, it would seem, of giving straight answers to plain
questions.[4]

The growing and necessary specialisation within
theology must lead to the development of particular
methods of study and analysis appropriate for each discipline. But the Church's theologians need always to ensure
that these theological tools do not become 'machinery' seen
as an end in itself, rather than a part of the overarching
quest for 'perfection', of telling the whole truth about God.
It may be timely to revisit some theologians of an earlier
age, whose life and work demonstrate the concern for cath-
olicity articulated by Cyril of Jerusalem, and who are
examples of an integrative approach to the Christian tradition. We will concentrate below on the Anglican divines
of the sixteenth and seventeenth centuries and those influenced by them, but we will note first of all that these figures
were themselves heirs to a theological tradition that sought
an integrated vision of God. The Early Fathers, the medieval Scholastics and the Renaissance Humanists were not
independent thinkers who specialised in one branch of
theology, but individuals working within an ecclesial community who attempted to make sense of the whole
theological enterprise, telling the whole truth about God.

It might be objected that this approach to theology is
unhelpful, if not impossible today. Theological studies have
so developed since the time of the Caroline Divines that
the possibilities for integration open to them are no longer
available to us. The diversity of material produced by
writers such as Richard Hooker, Lancelot Andrewes and
Jeremy Taylor is certainly impressive: from sermons to polemical tracts; from catechesis for communicants to
theological treatises; from books of moral guidance to
prayers for liturgical and private use. But it was possible at
the turn of the seventeenth century to possess a reasonable
grasp of all the theological disciplines as they were then
understood, while to try to emulate the range of learning
of the Caroline Divines in our own day would be mere
dilettantism.

It is not my intention to argue below that Hooker, Andrewes *et al* should inspire today's theologians to produce a twentieth century *summa*, nor to undervalue the detailed work undertaken by theological specialists. But in the light of the fragmentation that so characterises the contemporary theological scene, the integrative tradition may yet have some important insights to offer about a theological style that can provide a more inclusive, if less defined, vision of God, and which has implications for the way in which the Christian tradition may be developed and renewed. In particular we may note three important and closely related features of the integrative tradition: the integration of theology and spirituality, the integration of thought and feeling, and the integration of the arts with theological discourse. In each of these areas, the integrative tradition challenges us to see things whole, by its suggestion that theology is an activity of the whole person, not only the detached analytical self at home in the world of doctrinal precision, but also the emotionally engaged praying Christian happy to work theologically in the imaginative, evocative and imprecise world of the poet and the artist.

We can see all three features at work in the prayers of Lancelot Andrewes. His *Preces Privatae* were not intended for publication, and, when the manuscript was discovered, much of it was on scraps of paper that had been covered with the tears of its author. Yet this great emotion was accompanied by a profound intellectual process. Andrewes generally prayed with a pen in his hand and nine or ten books on the shelf beside him, writing down the prayer as he prayed. It was his belief that God should be addressed not in one's own words, but in the language of Scripture and the Christian tradition. In his wrestling with that tradition through a process that was both thinking and praying, the tradition itself was further developed.

T. S. Eliot's description of the quality of Andrewes' sermons reflects the same concern with spirituality, feeling and the poetic use of language through which new theological truth may be conveyed:

> To persons whose minds are habituated to feed on the vague jargon of our time, when we have a vocabulary for everything and exact ideas about nothing . . . when the language of theology itself . . . tends to become a language of tergiversation – Andrewes may seem pedantic and verbal. It is only when we have saturated ourselves in his prose, followed the movement of his thought, that we find his examination of words terminating in an ecstasy of assent. Andrewes takes a word and derives a world from it, squeezing and squeezing the word until it yields a full juice of meaning which we should never have supposed any word to possess.[5]

Eliot recognises in Andrewes the authority of one who approaches his task having integrated his faculties of thinking and feeling. This enables him in turn to fulfil what Eliot describes as the task of the poet, itself a process of the integration of various elements. In his essay, 'The Metaphysical Poets', Eliot describes the poet's creative process in these terms:

> When a poet's mind is perfectly equipped for its work, it is constantly amalgamating disparate experience; the ordinary man's experience is chaotic, irregular, fragmentary. The latter falls in love, or reads Spinoza, and these two experiences have nothing to do with each other, or with the noise of the typewriter or the smell of cooking; in the mind of the poet these experiences are always forming new wholes.[6]

This was one of the characteristic features of the poetry of Donne and Herbert that so annoyed Samuel Johnson: 'The most heterogeneous ideas are yoked by violence together.'[7] Most modern critics would admit the heterogeneity, but deny that 'yoked by violence' was a fair description of the general effect. At its best the Metaphysical conceit[8] communicates a unified experience of sensation, emotion and thought:

> Donne does not merely examine his theme academically and from a safe distance, articulating its various parts at leisure. He *experiences* it, in the mind and 'on the pulses', in all its exact sensory connotations. Ideas, theories, doctrines, quotations,

allusions, imagery are all devoted to this end, they are inherent, all caught up in the intensity of the emotion.[9]

Here is George Herbert on prayer, conveying the numinous richness of the subject by a cumulative use of mutually incompatible images:

Prayer the Churches banquet, Angels age,
      Gods breath in man returning to his birth,
      The soul in paraphrase, heart in pilgrimage,
The Christian plummet sounding heav'n and earth;

Engine against th'Almightie, sinners towre,
      Reversed thunder, Christ-side-piercing spear,
      The six-daies world-transposing in an houre,
A kinde of tune, which all things heare and fears;

Softnesse, and peace, and joy, and love, and blisse,
      Exalted Manna, gladnesse of the best,
      Heaven in ordinarie, man well drest,
The milkie way, the bird of Paradise,

      Church-bels beyond the starres heard, the souls bloud,
      The land of spices; something understood.[10]

The chief advantage of the poetic conceit as employed by Herbert and John Donne is the quality of inclusiveness it makes possible. It is a way of bringing into poetry all their interests, activities, and speculations. No part of experience is regarded as intrinsically unpoetical; all is equally available in the act of composition. This inclusiveness is a direct result of their religious conviction that the whole world can be seen as a sacrament of God's presence. Rowan Williams encourages us to see this as a fundamental characteristic of a Catholic tradition, which he describes in terms of our response to a work of art:

Our tradition . . . has struggled in word, image and ritual to say what is involved in the conviction that the spirit of Jesus in the community makes the stuff of the material world transparent to God's act, the material of sacramental grace. It has done all this ultimately with the delight we might have in looking again and again at a picture or a drama that has moved and changed us,

enlarged our world, seeing more and more dimensions and connections.[11]

Seeing connections, seeing life steadily and seeing it
whole: this quest for an integrated vision is a tradition of
which the Caroline Divines are prime exemplars, but it
occurs in other places and at other times. Often it is characterised by one or more of the qualities we have noted
above: the integration of theology and spirituality, of
thought and feeling, of the work of the artist with that
of the theologian. Within the Anglican tradition we might
mention the Cambridge Platonists, for whom union with
God was the goal both of philosophy and faith, through the
merging of the rational and the spiritual, and who studied
nature together with Scripture as the two books of the
works of God. A little later there is Samuel Johnson, learned
and witty writer and critic and devout Christian believer,
who would visit St Clement's Church to read the Collect of
the Day four or five times, return home to write his own
prayer based on the collect, then visit the church again to
pray over it. A hundred years later the tradition has as
its representatives the Cambridge trio of biblical scholars,
Lightfoot, Westcott and Hort, of whom Gordon Wakefield
comments: 'Their scholarly rigour was grounded in faith
and devotion. They approached the Scriptures with an awe
inspired by the long tradition of reverence to Christ and
personal piety. There was no great gulf between the
asceticism of the study and the asceticism of the cell.'[12]
Within our own century further examples of an integrative
tradition come to mind: Kenneth Kirk, moral theologian,
allegorising preacher, and writer on Christian spirituality;
John Burnaby, whose Hulsean Lectures *Amor Dei* and his
later essay on 'Christian Prayer' in *Soundings* combine theological enquiry with an analysis of the spiritual life; Austin
Farrer, theologian, philosopher and classicist, who wrote of
artistic invention that it 'probably casts as much light as
anything human on God's devising of the world',[13] and
whose own sermons are rich with poetic images and inter-
spersed with original verses.[14] Such a tradition is happy to
accept the analogy of H. E. Root in *Soundings*: 'Believers are

in love, theologians write love-poems and metaphysicians – natural theologians – write criticisms of poetry.'[15] More recently still, Andrew Louth's book *Discerning the Mystery*[16] unites theology, spirituality and liturgy, and praises the poetic approach to tradition through the use of allegory.

From within the Roman Catholic tradition, a similar synthesis of theology, philosophy, aesthetics and contemplation is achieved by Hans Urs von Balthasar in his theological aesthetics *The Glory of the Lord*.[17] Its reviewer in *The Church Times* described it as 'the kind of work which renews one's whole understanding of what the theological enterprise is', allowing us 'to re-appropriate the living tradition of the church at a time when many are feeling cut-off from it.' Balthasar approaches the words, actions and sufferings of Jesus as presented in the New Testament as an aesthetic unity, held together by the 'style' of unconditional love. Through Christ, the love which God *is* shines through to the world. This is Balthasar's basic intuition, and it is an intuition which runs counter to the prevailing tendency of his contemporaries to use the paraphernalia of gospel criticism to tear into fragments what is an obvious unity. As Balthasar himself comments:

> One may . . . fear that the present volume will appear methodologically imprecise to the reader who is a professional theologian – indeed, that it will strike him as hopelessly amateurish, for many dividing-lines that have become customary are not observed (they are frequently a hindrance, when one wishes to have an overview of the whole phenomenon which is being treated).[18]

When that 'phenomenon' is the glory of God in the face of Jesus Christ, only a contemplative aesthetic reading of the New Testament is adequate, only an integrative approach can begin to tell the whole truth about the mystery that is God:

> religion is something very different from an optimus modus vivendi: we want fire and mystery and extasis, and the relation of every slightest thing to God in some mysterious way. It is here that the saint and the artist have much to teach.[19]

The words are those of Bishop George Bell, whose writings and ministry provide a striking example of one who sought to see life whole. On first meeting him, Martin Browne, who was to become Bell's Diocesan Director of Religious Drama, was captivated by Bell's 'youthfulness which had nothing to do with years', the pressure of a handshake that 'denoted his secret strength and his tremendous warmth of heart', and a rare and intense interest in the other's opinions which Browne discovered was due to 'a tremendous breadth of interests, and a breadth of mind too, which operated in every direction.'[20] Bell was convinced that the arts could make a major contribution to theology and the life of the Church in an age which was becoming increasingly obsessed with efficiency and the need to define and distinguish. In terms very reminiscent of Matthew Arnold, he defended his conviction in his last speech to the Upper House of the Convocation of Canterbury, asserting that people paid

> far too much heed to economists, bankers, engineers, directors, business men and politicians and far too little attention to poets, philosophers, painters, sculptors, novelists of imagination, writers, teachers, musicians, even ballet dancers and every form of artist.[21]

Bell's motivation for attacking the morality of the area bombing policy during the Second World War was based in part on ethical arguments and his interpretation of what constituted a just war. But it also sprang from his sense of horror that so many cultural artefacts were being destroyed, artefacts which would be required as resources for recivilising a defeated Germany.[22] The work of artistic creation was for Bell a significant way in which men and women could enlarge their vision of God and in which the Christian tradition could be developed and renewed for each generation.

A twentieth-century poet who shared Bell's insight as well as his friendship was T. S. Eliot, who as a critic had much praise for earlier representatives of an integrative tradition, and contributed to that tradition through his own creative work. It should come as no surprise that one contemporary critic found the same qualities in Eliot's poetry that the latter admired in the work of Donne and Herbert:

> to take, in any measure, what Mr Eliot's poetry has to give is to be educated into a new understanding of the nature of precision in thought, and at the same time to experience intimately an emotional and spiritual discipline. And this holds, irrespective of whether or not the reader subscribes to Christian doctrine.[23]

Leavis' last sentence suggests that poetry has the capacity to communicate religious truth that is not dependent on doctrinal formulation, but available to anyone who reads with attention and openness. It raises an important question about the relationship between the creative freedom of the artist and the doctrinal constraints of the Christian tradition and thus about precisely how we are to integrate them into a single vision. The same tension is present in Bell's thinking about doctrine and aesthetics. While insisting that the Christian artist should always work within the framework of the doctrinal requirements of the Church, he recognised too the autonomy of the artist in moulding the tradition. In a famous consistory court judgement, Bell defended the artist's right to invent, change and improvise to the very end of the act of creation, for 'only thus can he achieve that quality of spontaneity, freshness and immediacy which belongs to the total work of art.' How such spontaneity, freshness and immediacy are to be incorporated in a work of art that is to teach doctrine is a tension that is not satisfactorily resolved. George Herbert may provide his work with a didactic gloss – 'A verse may find him, who a sermon flies,/And turn delight into a sacrifice'[24] – but poetry, music and art have their own integrity that is not always easily malleable into the service of systematic theology.

This is not a new tension: the Fathers taught us to prefer abstract terms, and saw their task as defining and refining, of drawing boundaries between what was right and wrong. But most of those responsible for the Scriptures, the foundational documents of the Christian faith that the patristic writers were seeking to interpret, were not in the business of providing definitions and distinctions. They were

67

creative artists, poets and story-tellers, whose language was designed to evoke, to conjure up pictures in the mind of the listener, making large demands upon the imagination.[25]

The process of evoking, of conjuring up pictures, is of necessity an imprecise process, and a story or poem is a fragile and vulnerable instrument, a delicate construction of the mind with little to protect it, with no guarantees as to how it may be interpreted. It is striking, therefore, that this seems to have been a characteristic method of Jesus himself in his teaching. Christopher Evans comments:

> The man who chooses to talk consistently in parables must surely recognize that in doing so he is putting himself and the truth at risk, and if he lives to see what is done with his parables he is likely to find himself from time to time expostulating: 'Clumsy oaf! That is not what I said or meant at all.' Nevertheless, he may still maintain that for all its fragility no other instrument will do for the particular subject in hand.[26]

Evans' essay on 'Parable and Dogma' is instructive in a consideration of a way of doing theology that seeks to find a place for the poetic as well as the kerygmatic, for it acknowledges the presence of both kinds of material within the Gospel tradition itself and asks questions about how they are to be related one to another.

> The language of parable is analogical and suggests; the language of theology is substantial and states. The language of parable is random, being drawn from here and there in human life; it is light of touch, indirect in manner, oblique in reference, delivering a glancing blow at its object... The language of kerygma... goes beyond this and belongs to the privileged vocabulary of theology; it is heavy in character, direct in reference, and aims to secure its object.

When parable is pressed too harshly into the service of a kerygmatic theology, it is in danger of losing its very nature as parable, thus violating the intention and destroying the mystery of Jesus' dominant mode of discourse, a mystery that conveys the mystery of the Kingdom as it describes it.

How then are the two modes of language and theology to be related? One solution to the tension between them, the solution proposed by Dodd and Jeremias, is questioned by Evans. Dodd and Jeremias had both proposed that the main point of the parables, once shorn of later moralising conclusions and allegorical elements, was to comment upon and defend some particular aspect of the basic message of Jesus as it could be constructed from elsewhere in the Gospel material. In other words, the parable assists, substantiates or defends the dogma. Evans questions this conclusion on form-critical grounds, demonstrating that 'whatever the subsequent use made of parable in the tradition, it is not obvious, nor perhaps likely, that it elects itself as a form of utterance for proclaiming an eschatological message or for defending it.'[27]

For an alternative explanation, Evans turns to the literary-critical approach to the study of the parables which was becoming increasingly widespread at the time his lecture was delivered.[28] Such an approach argues for the relative autonomy of the parables as internal organic unities of form and content apart from any immediate reference to anything outside themselves. Parabolic or metaphorical language is not 'an ornamental form of expression for what could be equally well or even better said otherwise', but something much more significant. If the insights of this school of thought are correct, then the parabolic/non-discursive/poetical has a vital role to play in the continuing renewal of the Christian tradition. For by reading the parables without asking the questions that one usually asks of texts written in the conceptual and univocal language of discursive reason, but rather with an imaginative attention that is more characteristic of contemplative prayer, comes new understanding and new vision:

> Insight and understanding of existence proceed from movements of the imagination which take shape in fresh combinations of words whereby they can convey more than they ordinarily do. Parable . . . involves a coherent and self-contained organization of form and content through which something is seen anew.[29]

The parables, then, will not fit neatly into a narrowly defined doctrinal scheme. Evans suggests that the evangelists were unable to use them in this way, and we should

69

also try to keep them apart, allowing each kind of utterance to have its own force, seeing in the parables of Jesus 'an inducement of men . . . to a way of perception, and so perhaps to parables of their own'.[30] For whatever the precise connection between the parabolic/poetic and the doctrinal/discursive methods of doing theology, there seems good evidence to suggest that both are present in the teaching of Jesus, and therefore related in that they come at whatever remove from a single person, 'and to be unified in thought is part of the definition of being a person.'[31] Evans draws out the implications of this for New Testament study, that it is essential to explore these two types of material and see how they need each other if we are ever fully to understand the New Testament. But his conclusion also has implications for the whole theological enterprise, calling us to recognise the place within the development of doctrine and the renewal of the tradition of what has been described above as parabolic, and which shares with poetry, story, the arts and certain forms of prayer qualities of evocativeness, imagination and imprecision. As both modes of theology find a unity within the teaching of Jesus, so, it might be argued, should they be held in tension by the contemporary theologian and the contemporary Church. Only together can they lead to the ability to tell the whole truth about God, about humanity, and about the relationships within and between them, for the nature of a relationship cannot be captured in the logical terms of a propositional faith. The Church has not been altogether successful in holding these two modes together: the need to define, to make precise has often been pursued to the detriment of the imaginative mode.

In describing the tradition of theology beginning with the Caroline Divines, we have already noted that one of the characteristics displayed by its members was the ability to fuse thought and feeling, the poetic and the discursive together. The propensity of this tradition within Anglicanism to produce poets, artists and musicians has often been commented upon. There is evidently something within this tradition which activates and transforms the human imagination. I would argue that it is closely related

to the reticence within Anglicanism, although not exclusively there, narrowly to define belief. This characteristic is
partly an accident of history.

Stephen Sykes provides a helpful discussion of the
history of the distinction between things necessary to salvation and things indifferent in his chapter on the
fundamentals of Christianity in *The Study of Anglicanism*.[32]
He contrasts Erasmus' assertion that Christians needed to
agree upon a few simple truths for Christian living and
leave other matters open to debate with Luther's belief that
the whole Christian faith revealed in the Scriptures hung
together. The concept of things indifferent became an
important element in Hooker's defence of the Elizabethan
Settlement.[33] The Christian faith is portrayed as having a
hard skeleton and very soft flesh, which could be moulded
by the Prince more or less at will, without endangering the
integrity of the skeletal Gospel. On all indifferent things,
which in Hooker's analysis covers a large range of faith and
practice, Christians ought to defer to royal authority.[34] This
is in marked contrast to the Roman Catholic and Calvinist
view that Christianity amounted to a very full code,
invalidated if anything were removed. Jeremy Taylor, too,
argued that it is sufficient to believe in salvation by Christ
alone to be saved, and while other doctrines may be
deduced from this central one, they cannot be claimed as
articles of faith. If the Church tries to add to the central articles of belief, to make belief more comprehensive, it has the
effect of rendering belief narrower and more exclusive, and
possible even false and tyrannical.[35] The Elizabethan Settlement may well have been entirely a matter of political
expediency, and toleration a result of the unenforceability
of uniformity, but it *looked* like moderation and had the
appearance of tempering the excesses of spiritual
authority.[36] Where there is this sense of spiritual reticence,
where the heavy hand of Scripture or the magisterium is
lightened, then there develops an openness within a theological tradition to the insights of the arts, the imagination
and the life of prayer. These aspects of what has been
described above as an integrative tradition are one facet of
what Henry McAdoo describes as the 'polarity or quality

of living tension' characteristic of Anglican theological method:

> Beneath the surface was the feeling for the *via media* which was not in its essence compromise or an intellectual expedient, but a quality of thinking, an approach in which elements usually regarded as mutually exclusive were seen in fact to be complementary. These things were held in a living tension, not in order to walk the tight-rope of compromise, but because they were seen to be mutually illuminating and to fertilise each other.[37]

At the heart of this tension and acting as a unifying faculty was what Hooker called reason, based on an idea of reasonable law, which he believed to be seen in the workings of God and through all creation.[38] Despite an increasing tendency in his day to limit reason to the realm of the sciences, Taylor follows Hooker in propounding its integrative role:

> By reason, I do not mean a distinct topic, but a transcendent that runs through all topics; for reason, like logic, is instrument of all things else; and when revelation and philosophy, and public experience, and all other grounds of probability or demonstration have supplied us with matter, then reason does but make use of them.[39]

In Hooker's famous passage in praise of music, the work of art itself acts as the integrative medium, uniting thought and feeling, contemplative reason and sensory perception, in a process which is able to change the listener:

> Touching musical harmony whether by instrument or voice . . . so pleasing effects it hath in that very part of man which is most divine, that some have been thereby induced to think that the soul itself by nature is or hath in it harmony . . . The reason hereof is an admirable facility which music hath to express and represent to the mind, more inwardly than any sensible mean, the very standing, rising, and falling, the very steps and inflections every way, the turns and varieties of all passions whereunto the mind is subject; yea so to imitate them, that whether it resemble unto us the same state wherein our minds already are,

or a clean contrary, we are not more contentedly by the one confirmed, than changed and led away by the other. In harmony the very image and character even of virtue and vice is perceived, the mind delighted with their resemblances, and brought by having them often iterated into a love of the things themselves ... [Some music] carrieth as it were into ecstasies, filling the mind with an heavenly joy and for the time in a manner severing it from the body.[40]

Seeing life whole, telling the whole truth about God – the quest for an integrative vision of God is as urgent today as it has ever been. Our society is one increasingly beset by excessive certitude and reductive truth, in which we uncritically manage our small perceptual fields, and in which human identity is so often defined in terms of the work people do. Trying to see the tradition as a whole, including those parts of it which have been characterised above as poetic, parabolic, intuitive and contemplative, does not make for doctrinal precision, but rather for untidiness and vagueness, although it may be that the capacity to be vague is very important in the age of the sound-byte and the spin-doctor. It does demand a willingness to listen to others who do not share our particular specialism, and to be surprised and delighted when their insights modify our own thinking. It reminds us, contrary to the spirit of the age, that the Christian tradition is enriched and renewed not so much by further self-definition as by a flexible, open-hearted, poetic approach to life that is akin to the theological virtue of love, that which can 'bind everything together and complete the whole'.[41] Thomas Traherne described love as 'the Greatest of all Principles ... [which] will break in evry where, as that without which the World could not be enjoyed.'[42] Elsewhere he provides us with a poetic vision of its integrative and unifying power:

> Transcendent Objects doth my God provide,
> In such convenient Order all contriv'd,
>> That All things in their proper place
>>> My soul doth best embrace,
>> Extends its Arms beyond the Seas,
>> Abov the Hevens its self can pleas,

> With God enthron'd may reign:
> Like sprightly Streams
> My Thoughts on Things remain;
> Ev'n as som vital Beams
> They reach to, shine on, quicken Things, and make
> Them truly Usefull; while I *All* partake.[43]

The Christian tradition likewise will continue to be truly useful, capable of being quickened into new insights and fresh discoveries, if and only if its teachers and learners are committed to seeing all things in their proper place, telling the whole truth about God, seeing life steadily and seeing it whole.

Notes to Chapter 3

1 Matthew Arnold, *To a Friend* from *The Strayed Reveller* (1849).
2 Matthew Arnold, *Culture and Anarchy: An Essay in Political and Social Criticism*, ed. J. Dover Wilson (Cambridge 1932), p. 50
3 Ibid., p. 48.
4 C. F. Evans, 'Parable and Dogma' from *Explorations in Theology* 2 (SCM, 1977).
5 T. S. Eliot, 'For Lancelot Andrewes' (1927), p. 16.
6 T. S. Eliot, 'The Metaphysical Poets' (1921) from *Selected Essays* (1932).
7 Samuel Johnson, 'Cowley' from *Lives of the Poets* (1779).
8 'Metaphysical' is a term popularised by Samuel Johnson to describe the tendency of Donne and Herbert to use some of the concepts of scholastic philosophy. 'Conceit' is here a technical word meaning a far-fetched comparison employed for poetic effect.
9 Gilbert Phelps, 'The Prose of Donne and Browne', from *The Pelican Guide to English Literature Vol. 3* (Penguin, 1956).
10 George Herbert, 'Prayer' (1) from *The English Poems of George Herbert*, ed. Patrides (Dent, 1974).
11 Rowan Williams, 'Teaching the Truth' from *Living Tradition*, ed. Jeffrey John (DLT, 1992), p. 34.
12 Gordon S. Wakefield, 'Anglican Spirituality' from *Christian Spirituality – Post Reformation and Modern*, ed. Louis Dupré and Don E. Saliers (SCM, 1989).
13 Austin Farrer, *Love Almighty and Ills Unlimited*.
14 Farrer, *Said or Sung* (Faith Press, 1960).
15 H. E. Root, 'Beginning All Over Again' from *Soundings* (Cambridge, 1962).
16 Andrew Louth, *Discerning the Mystery* (OUP, 1983).

17 Hans Urs von Balthasar, *The Glory of the Lord* (T. & T. Clark, 1989).
18 Ibid., Volume VII, p. 9.
19 George Bell to Hans Feibusch, 31 October 1941, Bell Papers, Vol. 151 f.18.
20 Quoted in R. C. D. Jasper, *George Bell, Bishop of Chichester* (Oxford, 1967).
21 *Chronicle of Convocation*, 1958, pp. 81–87.
22 For a fuller discussion of this point, see Giles Watson, Ph.D. thesis, Chapter 5: *Traditionalism and Dissent*.
23 F. R. Leavis, 'Christian Discrimination' from *The Common Pursuit* (1952).
24 George Herbert, 'The Church-Porch' from Patrides, op. cit.
25 For a fuller discussion of this point, and some contemporary stories loosely based on Scripture that demonstrate it, see Trevor Dennis, *Speaking of God* (SPCK, 1992).
26 Evans, op. cit., p. 127.
27 Ibid., p. 130.
28 The Ethel M. Wood Lecture for 1976.
29 Evans, op. cit., p. 132. For an extended discussion and numerous examples of this characteristic of works of art, see David Shearlock, *When Words Fail* (Canterbury Press, 1996).
30 Evans, op. cit., p. 136.
31 Ibid.
32 Ed. Stephen Sykes and John Booty (SPCK, 1988).
33 Richard Hooker, *Of the Laws of Ecclasiastical Polity* (OUP, 1845).
34 Ibid., Preface, III-V.
35 Jeremy Taylor, *The Liberty of Prophesying* (1650).
36 For a further discussion of this point, see Paul Avis, 'What is Anglicanism?' from Sykes and Booty, op. cit.
37 H. R. McAdoo, *The Spirit of Anglicanism* (Black, 1965), quoted by Avis.
38 See, e.g., Hooker, op. cit., III.viii.11.
39 Taylor, op. cit.
40 Hooker, op. cit, V.xxxviii.1.
41 Col. 3:14 (REB).
42 Traherne, 'The Fourth Century', paragraph 61 from *Centuries*.
43 Traherne, 'Hosanna', from *Elizabethan and Jacobean Poets* (Penguin, 1950).

4 Fixing the Fathers

Leslie Houlden

William Chillingworth was a Fellow of Trinity College, Oxford, who, in 1628, worried by the outcome of the English Church Settlement, became a Roman Catholic and went abroad to the Low Countries; but he speedily repented and returned to England and its established Church. In 1638 he published *The Religion of Protestants a Safe Way to Salvation*, a polemical work, as much theological writing has always been, but, in a period when the 'Bible and Fathers' formula was becoming established as a coherent basis for Anglicanism,[1] it struck a blow for a wider and more tolerant approach to religious authority. His most famous statement, 'The Bible I say, the Bible only is the religion of Protestants', looks like good traditional Reformation doctrine or perhaps sheer biblicism, but in fact it was part of a sustained argument for minimising the scope of definition in religion, certainty being hard to come by, and for leaving as much room as possible for the mind and conscience of the believer to operate upon the basic data of faith. Among the factors which led him to this proto-Latitudinarian position was the recognition that the appeal to the Fathers lacked the comforting stability that some of his fellow Anglicans attributed to it. In their eyes (and the conviction was still reflected in some of the more traditional degree syllabuses into the second half of this century), to settle religion on the dual basis of the Bible and the Fathers, with the latter serving as the authoritative tool of interpretation for the former (especially via the classic creeds), was as much as to say that the Church of England was more Catholic in its identity than other churches of the Reformation, for whom the principle of 'Scripture alone' ruled. It was therefore a prime element in establishing the claim to walk a *via media* between the extremes regrettably found in other communions.

Chillingworth, imbued with a liberal spirit of moral rationality, was moved in part towards that spirit by the recognition that 'the Fathers' (by then an Anglican term of growing currency) constituted no uniform body of teaching but disagreed among themselves, so that it was a case of one Father against another Father.[2] Even the great conciliar settlements of Nicea, Constantinople, Ephesus and Chalcedon were not quite what they seemed but concealed sharp and persisting conflicts and wide differences of understanding.[3] Moreover, opinions that in due course acquired the taint of heresy were to be found large as life in the writings of the most revered of the ancient teachers. In other words, the hallowed sense of the ship of orthodoxy, self-contained and entire, able to fight off heretical marauders, did scant justice to a complex history in which matters were a good deal more fraught, a good deal less tidy. For Chillingworth, the Bible itself was less an infallible authority than a standard against which faith was to be measured: the Scriptures were 'the pillars and supporters of Christian liberty'[4] and contained the message on which the Christian's 'mind must work'.[5] More ambitiously, he believed that if Christians could agree on this fundamental and simple approach, unity among them would ensue.[6]

This preference for Scripture (modified as it was by Chillingworth) went back, of course, to the roots of the Reformation, and radical Reformers had long concluded that the main doctrinal achievements of the patristic period (the Trinity and Chalcedonian Christology) were not luminously present in Scripture and could only with difficulty, and certainly not with assurance, be read from the biblical text. In England and on the Continent, many had suffered for this revolutionary discovery, most notably Servetus in Calvin's Geneva.[7] Though the intellectual and religious ethos of these people was very different from the wide-minded rationalism of Chillingworth, they shared a perception of Christian tradition which both drove a wedge between Scripture and the Fathers and depressed the stock of the latter, relativising them in relation to the total picture of Christian faith. A question-mark was put, a note of caution sounded, against even the most revered ancient interpreters of Scripture, who reckoned to have derived their doctrines from precisely that source.

It cannot be said that the questions implicit in this new situation have ever been satisfactorily answered. They have, moreover, acquired new shapes and dimensions in recent times, mostly adding to their intractability. But it is remarkable how tenacious the main lines of dispute have turned out to be. In the most general terms, it is the question of what status to give to patristic theology in the whole story of Christian belief and teaching. In many respects, the question is precisely the same for any other part of that story, from then until now. Are we to work with a picture of a succession of relatively homogeneous bodies of thought, doubtless including variations and even conflict but nevertheless, at least in hindsight, having a measure of shared assumptions and cultural unity; or with a picture, essentially teleological in character, that sees each succeeding episode as part of a cumulative whole? On the latter view, whatever the twists and turns, each builds on what preceded and contributes to what follows, so that a single structure is gradually constructed through time, within the life of the continuing Christian community; or else (in a less finite metaphor) a coherent journey is in progress, even though its end (in terms of human thought and language) remains beyond our ken.

In certain respects, the two approaches, synchronic and diachronic, can live happily side by side, as serving distinct purposes or as simply viewing the same material from different angles; but the more sharply the various synchronic pictures are defined in the mind, the more strongly the differences between them and the inner consistency of each (only partial though it may be, as we shall see) are likely to be apprehended. Then attempts to view them as contributions to a single intellectual enterprise may seem to be acts of violence done to the evidence. Yet the fact remains that, empirically and with whatever degree of make-believe, all have contributed to a single process and have

overwhelmingly been seen in that light and used for that
end. At the very least, they have arisen within the continuous and identifiable life of the Christian community.
The singleness of the total process dominates our thinking,
understandably so – whatever other perspectives we may
also entertain.

There is a modification when, as with the radical
Reformers we referred to earlier, the present reckons to base
itself on the appeal to a certain part of the distant past
(in their case Christian origins, or rather Scripture as their
inspired verbal embodiment), leaping over the intervening
episodes as of inferior value and authority, and frequently
positively erroneous. The attempt at fidelity to the biblical
model (or, with others, to the Early Church) can reproduce
only limited aspects of the matter in question (it is not
done by time-capsule), and it is inevitably coloured by the
interests and context of the later period. Witness, for
example, the varied so-called reproductions of early liturgical practice or early ministerial patterns.[8] No amount of
ecclesiastical grease-paint can turn a sixteenth or twentieth-
century bishop into a replica of Ignatius of Antioch or
Cyprian of Carthage; nor can the modern Church, 'staging'
the Eucharist, turn suburban congregations into replicas of
those that first used the rites that survive from the Early
Church. It is not hard to see that both synchronic and diachronic appreciations, the one letting the past be the past,
the other seeing it as contributing to a long process down
to the present, defy these deliberate attempts to obliterate
time and development.

Nevertheless, with all the differences between them, both
the radical Reformers and the likes of Chillingworth were
putting the Fathers in a new relativised light. In effect, and
only embryonically, they were initiating the long process
that was to lead to the possibility of the synchronic view of
Christian doctrine and pose a problematic alternative to the
tenacious diachronic perception.[9]

It may help to consider examples. The synchronic
approach to Christian doctrine (in a central aspect, belief
about Jesus) is well seen in Jaroslav Pelikan's *Jesus through
the Centuries* (1985). We are given 18 different ways in which

Jesus has been perceived and believed in over a wide range of historical and cultural settings. Of course, not all of them involve explicit differences of formal doctrine – many would happily sign up to the Definition of Chalcedon – but each is implicitly the purveyor of a different mode of belief, and, in that important sense, of a different doctrine. Yet, with this achieved, the book disappoints in the formidable task left to the abandoned reader: What then are *we* to believe? The modern Christian, contemplating the variegated past, revealed in its diversity, is left wondering where a comprehensible heritage of faith is to be found, or else on precisely what basis modern developments can be made. There may be a dizzy sense of a doctrinal anarchy beneath the cloak of institutional continuity.

Contrast Wolfhart Pannenberg's well-established *Jesus, God and Man* (1968), in which, not untypically, the patristic doctrine of the Trinity is taken for granted, as is the doctrine of Christ as divine-human, even though, for all his orthodox assumptions, Pannenberg is seriously critical of the particular form in which the latter was articulated in the Chalcedonian era and expounds the merits and drawbacks of various forms that the orthodox doctrine has taken at different stages of Christian history. These accounts of historical variations, and Pannenberg's own preferred account (centring on the resurrection as crucial to Christology),[10] are presented as standing comfortably within a broadly unitary process of development. Whatever the inadequacies at this point or that of the various formulations given to Christology, the impression we receive is of a doctrine fundamentally single and secure which, for reasons of human failure to guard against inappropriateness of statement, has often been misleadingly formulated.

The relativising (and in effect diminishing, or, at the least, sceptically interrogating) of the Fathers which was, to varying degrees, explicit in the scriptural concentration of the sixteenth-century Reformers and again in the horizon-wideners like Chillingworth in the seventeenth, has been put in a much more searching light with the rise of biblical criticism. Despite resistance from some styles of New Testament theology,[11] insisting on the direct power of biblical patterns of thought (though often with some difficulty), this has, in a whole battery of ways, amplified the synchronic understanding of the New Testament to such a deafening level that the Christian's reception of the text is bound to have an oblique character, simply by reason of distance and difference between then and now. The effect is then for the text to be perceived as suggestive rather than imperious, compelling those who receive it to make their own cooperative effort of understanding and imagination. Modern methods of New Testament study, whether they be redaction-critical, social-historical, or literary, have in common the capacity to affect the reader in this theologically demanding way. More still, they create an unmistakable sense of the diversity of Christian belief or response to Jesus already in the first decades: this was not, except at the most basic level, a homogeneous movement but diverse in its modes of thought – and well acquainted with internal controversy.

The effect of these methods of studying the foundation documents of Christian faith on the reception of those of the following period (usually, but with a degree of artificiality, taken as ending in the middle of the fifth century) is twofold. In the first place, it creates a certain expectation that the Fathers too are to be studied and understood along lines similar to those familiar in work on the New Testament. Secondly, it gives rise to the question of how one is to view the undoubted contrast, now all too plain to us, between the idioms of the New Testament and the various ways of thought of the subsequent 'episode', that of the Fathers, at any rate from the later years of the second century. As Chillingworth already recognised, the patristic 'mind' itself was far from unified, despite a number of important common intellectual and cultural assumptions. This in turn raises the question whether it is best to see the movement from the earlier to the later period in terms of 'development', implying some form of coherent movement or a process marked chiefly by elucidation or minor adaptation to context; or whether the differences are too great to be most naturally understood in those terms. Undoubtedly, the Fathers themselves saw their work in developmental

81

terms; or rather, they generally reckoned to be doing no more than reproducing or interpreting the Scriptures, both old and new. It is only the acute sensitising of our present-day synchronic faculties that makes us unhappy with their view of their work.[12] Undoubtedly too, we should not rush to think in terms of sealed-off periods: there was no sudden lurch at the end of the period covered by the writing of the New Testament books. Some of the second-century writers in particular live in a world similar to that of some of the later New Testament writers,[13] and the language of the Gospel of John seemed (but with misleading ease) to chime in with the thought of later Platonist Christians.

There is, however, still a difference between the procedures now widely accepted, not only in academic but also in church circles, as legitimate and helpful in the study of the New Testament writings, and the way in which the world of the Fathers is regarded. Consider the 1993 Vatican document, published with high authority, *The Interpretation of the Bible in the Church*.[14] The document outlines the numerous and diverse methods that have come to be used in the study of the Bible, by Catholic and Protestant scholars alike. All are accepted and commended for use,[15] subject to the very loosely stated proviso that, as far as believers are concerned, all is done within the context of faith. The effect is to recognise that in whole and in its parts, Scripture has no single meaning, and exegesis has no one legitimate outcome, hard to reach, perhaps, but in principle discoverable. Interpretation may involve suggesting a range of disparate meanings, corresponding to the varied questions that can be addressed to the text: relating to source, authorship, historical setting, social background, lexical sense, theological thought, or literary structure. Believers and unbelievers alike, readers are exposed to the text's multifaceted sense, and moved by it as by other writings capable of such rich enquiry – but, for believers, within the assumption of a common allegiance to Christ shared by New Testament writer and Christian reader alike.[16]

It is interesting that only the Roman Catholic Church (those with long memories might add 'of all churches') has issued such a comprehensive official analysis and endorsement of the principle of Scripture's multiple meanings. It is even more interesting to ask how easy it would be for that (or any other) Church to adopt a similar approach to the writings of the Fathers and their theological achievement; that is, to approach that crucial and formative era in Christian thought, epitomised in the authoritative creeds, from a similar range of standpoints. This would make abundantly plain the multiplicity of meanings which the patristic writings bear, and it would place them in their original contexts, as a necessary key to many of those meanings. There is now no shortage of contributions to work of this kind: see, for example, Peter Brown's life of Augustine of Hippo (1967) and Robin Lane Fox's *Pagans and Christians* (1986). But it is worth pondering how easy church authority would find it to sponsor an analysis and endorsement of the strictly synchronic, contextualised study of the theological developments of this period, which have proved so fundamental to the traditional dogmatic structure of orthodox Christianity. Seeing the Fathers synchronically, as Scripture has come to be seen, would create a comparable sense of indirectness, of critical reception, as both intellectual and historical contexts brought home the disjunctions between the patristic period and our own.

By way of example, let us take one of the central concerns of that period. It is well known that two distinct lines of thought or theological imagination contributed to the building up of the conviction of God as Trinity. Neither of them viewed candidly in context seems wholly compelling when seen from a modern standpoint.

The first, to be found chiefly but not exclusively in Latin Christianity, was rootedly monotheist but knew God as expressed through attributes and agents, the two not being wholly distinguished, thus modifying the divine solitariness. Jesus was the one concrete agent, but was himself understood by way of scriptural divine attributes (such as 'word' and 'wisdom') or personified figures ('son', 'angel') with whom he was identified. Once you adopted this procedure and let it run, your possibilities might seem, in theory, unbounded – or, at least, bounded only by the range of such images (attributes and agents of God) available in

Scripture. There seemed no reason in logic or in principle why Jesus might not be understood or illuminated in terms of any number of biblical attributes or facets of God: breath (spirit), countenance, arm, hand, face, rock, sacrifice-provider, husband-lover, shepherd, temple-presence . . . Many of these images had indeed figured, perhaps momentarily, in the early Christian imagination: New Testament passages spring to mind. Here was the material (again, in logic and in principle) for not a trinitarian idea of God but of one God surrounded with a multiplicity, a plethora of attributes or agents, ready, at a stirring of the imagination, to be turned into a heavenly 'population' of some magnitude – of some or any of which Jesus might, in certain circumstances or turns of language, be seen as the instrument or embodiment, or else indeed as himself one among the many.

That limits were placed on this luxuriance and that order was brought to the potential chaos seems to have been, at least in part, the effect of certain significant icons and formulas in early Christianity, such as the baptismal formula in Matthew 28:19 ('in the name of the Father and of the Son and of the Holy Spirit'), or the 'Grace' in 2 Corinthians 13:13, or the story of Jesus' baptism in Mark 1 (= Matt. 3 and Luke 3), where God has in association with himself just two figures – Jesus the Son and the Spirit: so that there was (not in logic or principle but in effect) a trinitarian outcome. Nevertheless, it was a Trinity which was rootedly monotheistic: it was the one God who, at a certain point in history (whether at the creation or in inspiring prophets or in the coming of Jesus) expressed himself in the figure of Jesus, as he also was experienced by way of his 'Spirit' (also moving between being a simple image/attribute of divine energy – God's breath or wind – and a personified agent after the manner of Isa. 55:11).

The second pattern, chiefly associated with Alexandrian Christianity, with its strong Platonist strain, was quite different, though it used some of the same materials. Here God, essentially 'other' than his universe, related to it, from the conceiving and executing of the creation onwards, by means of his eternal Word, seen not as one attribute among many but as the unique instrument of divine externality, the one all-sufficient mediator between God and all else: for what more could God require for such communication, whether for creation or for redemption? It was this eternal, personal Word that had donned 'flesh' (or humanness) as Jesus, thereby making himself accessible to the human race by an act of infinite and amazing condescension, evoking, with full propriety, the worship of all. In this binitarian pattern, where, as God's agent, he was wholly sufficient and omnicompetent, no room was left for further agents of God or (if one were to reach for such language) participants in the divine being. Both models could draw on Old Testament texts, though the second depended heavily on a certain reading of the scriptural wisdom literature and it owed much more to Platonism, through whose eyes it read that literature, and, for its Christian source, to the prologue of the Gospel of John.

How then did this logically compact binitarian doctrine ever land up in a belief in God as trinitarian (as it had by, at the latest, the second half of the fourth century)? To a large degree (though not exclusively) by the same sense of the normative and traditional character of basic Christian formulas that served to reduce the potential plethora of the first scheme to a trinity: here, increase; there, reduction. Result: a certain apparent consensus but, below the surface, an array of forces and texts that are likely to have a relativising effect on the modern observer and to put Christian thought about the being of God, as so defined, in a context demanding (shall we say?) circumspection. The procedures operating in both models belong to a world quite other than our own. None of this falsifies trinitarian belief *per se* (we shall see that there are other routes towards it), but it urges care in the lines of reasoning that may be used to support it.

This example[17] also puts into context the idea of Christ's pre-existence, which is both central to patristic conclusions on the Trinity and so problematic when it comes to giving now a convincing account of Christ's humanness in patristic terms – perhaps in any terms: how can so heavenly a one, so unconstrained in the centre of his being by our limitations, be human in a meaningful sense? Thereby it raises with some urgency the question of the place of the

85

patristic 'package' in the story of Christian thought. In its origins, as we saw, it was itself heavily dependent on categories derived from old and new Scriptures, used in ways that subserved the need to express the Christian conviction of the centrality of Jesus, seen without hesitation as adumbrated in seemingly propitious passages. But the appropriateness of texts was judged almost wholly at a purely verbal level, and there was rarely much attempt to enquire into original meanings and contexts; Scripture was pure text, not the reflection of innumerable situations of the distant past, as in modern study. Others, notably Jews, were keen to point out at the time that the texts bore no such sense; and modern critics, using the methods referred to above, and whether believers or not, are bound to agree. They might see a kind of poetic appropriateness, or even a broad providentiality, in this use of texts from the old Scriptures, but that is scarcely the spirit in which patristic writers used them and declared 'their meaning'.

If we turn to the other end of the patristic process, whether to Chalcedon in AD 451 or some other convenient point, we meet a comparable yet distinct problem. Whether we think of the perennially authoritative writings of Augustine and Jerome in the West or (for example) Basil and John Chrysostom in the East, or of succinct formulas of faith like the Apostles' and Niceno-Constantinopolitan Creeds, in due course liturgically inscribed on Christian minds, the patristic achievement was essentially unchallenged by mainstream Christian thinkers until recent centuries (we saw some sniping from the margins in the Reformation period). But that constant use and veneration concealed a process of reception that was far from passive. The Fathers were subject to selectivity, constructive interpretation (sometimes of a kind that would now be called deconstruction), and relocation in new intellectual contexts – a process of development, comparable to the Fathers' own treatment of Scripture, rarely wilful in its adaptive activity, and surely the necessary condition of the continuing vitality and utility of the patristic achievement. It is interesting that in the current academic enthusiasm for patristic orthodoxy, especially in trinitarian doctrine,[18] the aspect that is frequently seized upon is the so-called 'social' Trinity of the Cappadocian Fathers of the later fourth century, rather than, for example, the more (though not exclusively) monotheistic tendency of Augustine. It is hard not to think that this emphasis on God as the epitome and source of all community in his own inner being is not a response to a felt need to anchor the social and communal demands of the Gospel, and indeed the corresponding needs of modern societies, in the being of God himself. The trend can be put forward as drawing on the endless riches of the patristic heritage; or else it can be seen, more sceptically, as making the most of a fortuitously useful strand in the teaching of a group of thinkers whose concerns were quite other than the needs of late twentieth-century Christian theologians anxious about their churches and the fragmenting communities in which we live. Moreover, it is not easy to trace such a doctrine back beyond the Cappadocians, let alone to the New Testament, where it can find support only in the Gospel of John abstracted from its original context. Of course, none of this is to deny the Gospel desirability of the harmonious reconstruction of society, only to question some of the arguments drafted in support of it. It is indeed a matter on which many faiths make common cause, and it is perhaps a pity to suggest that Christianity has a monopoly of proper theological backing for it.

It used to be commonplace for the past to be interpreted in terms of the approved and desirable goal towards which it could be seen as tending; whether effortlessly or tortuously, perhaps with setbacks as well as advances. Present (and future) determined what was seen as significant in the past and how it was to be regarded. The desirable end might be parliamentary democracy or the establishment of Henry VIII's Church-State polity; it might be the triumph of a supposed master-race or simply the firm hand of the propertied on the tiller of society. The interpretative clarity which such a viewpoint yields is at the expense of the past's own integrity. Neither Magna Carta nor the work of Oliver Cromwell is most adequately seen as a providential step on the ineluctable march towards Gladstonian Liberalism or universal suffrage. Still less were Helena and Constantine, King Cole and King Arthur adumbrations of the Henrician Reformation of the English Church.[19] Each (supposing their historical reality) has to be interpreted in the context of his or her own age and in the light of the circumstances then obtaining. So much now seems clear and is generally admitted, so that groups importing the past nakedly into the present to determine and form it are commonly regarded as dangerously and foolishly atavistic. A belief can after all be formally identical from one person to another, or one period or culture to another, but when viewed in its total context and when the attempt is made to grasp the 'feel' of the belief and not just its ostensible and direct claim, then it soon becomes clear that one is dealing to all intents and purposes with a variety of beliefs, presenting themselves under the same reassuring label.[20]

In the interpretation of the Christian tradition, however, there are factors that lead to reluctance to shed a particular version of teleological theory. It is arguable indeed that the Judeo-Christian eschatological perspective, with its sense of a God-directed drive through history towards an intended end, is at the root of secular manifestations of purposive theory. But in Christianity the picture is radically modified by the constant looking back towards the reference point of Jesus as well as forwards towards a future consummation of God's purposes.[21] Combine this sense of two known points, one ascertainable in the New Testament writings, the other taken in faith, with the fact of an uninterrupted tradition of devotion and belief linking the two, and it is not in the least surprising that Christianity has worked with a strong insistence on the continuities at the expense of the recognition of differences, the diachronic at the expense of the synchronic. Modern historical awareness, whether applied to the New Testament period (with its own internal diversity) or indeed to any later eras, makes it more adequate to the evidence to think less in terms of traceable traditions, developing smoothly through history, with each period achieving its own clarifications and solutions and building on the fruits of earlier phases of development, and more in terms of a series of episodes in Christian tradition, of course linked, often with great complexity, to earlier and later episodes, but also in many respects discrete, each functioning on its own terms and with its own kind and measure of coherence.

Such a picture has the advantage of giving us a certain freedom from a misleading and unreasonable tyranny of the past and enabling us to respond to new demands without the need to feel an unjustified sense of betrayal of our predecessors in faith. At the same time, there is every reason to derive aid and stimulus from our forerunners by means of the greatest possible knowledge of their thought and manners; so long as we exercise our unique responsibility of discipleship under God and refrain from passing it over to 'the tradition', especially when such a move is congenial on other grounds. There is much to be said for the view that this is in fact how many Christians proceed and always have done. It is only a pity that they so often feel a need to camouflage their present response to God with appeals to ancient authorities, viewed through distorting lenses, sometimes as a distraction from responsible decision-making in answer to the needs of the God-given present.

Notes to Chapter 4

1 Taking a more positive view of the Fathers than, for example, Articles XIX–XXI of the Thirty-Nine Articles of 1562.
2 See Robert R. Orr, *Reason and Authority: the Thought of William Chillingworth* (Clarendon Press, 1967), p. 139; W. K. Jordan, *The Development of Religious Toleration in England* (Allen & Unwin, 1936), p. 385; also, and famously, G. L. Prestige, *Fathers and Heretics* (SPCK, 1948), p. 150, for St Cyril's view of St Theodoret.
3 So it was not so much that by scriptural standards they 'have erred', as Article XIX asserted, but that they were incoherent as a guide to faith.
4 Chillingworth, *The Religion of Protestants* ii.1; see Orr, op. cit., p. 113.
5 Orr, op. cit., p. 114.
6 Jordan, op. cit., pp. 379–400.
7 For England, see Diarmaid MacCulloch, *Thomas Cranmer* (Yale, 1996), pp. 145, 407. For Germany, see G. H. Williams, *The Radical Reformation* (Westminster Press, 1962).
8 See J. T. Burtchaell, *From Synagogue to Church* (Cambridge, 1992), chs.

1–4; R. A. Campbell, *The Elders* (T. & T. Clark, 1994), ch. 1; and more generally the seminal work, Robert L. Wilken, *The Myth of Christian Beginnings* (SCM, 1971).

9 MacCulloch (op. cit., p. 490) sees glimmerings of a more historical perception in the writings of Stephen Gardiner as against those of Cranmer.

10 Pannenberg has some discussion of a synchronic kind of the New Testament material on the resurrection, but with predictably confident and useful conclusions; especially when put alongside the many discussions from New Testament scholars who are working towards no wider picture, e.g. C. F. Evans, *Resurrection and the New Testament* (SCM, 1970), among many others.

11 For a valiant and sensitive attempt, see R. Morgan with J. Barton, *Biblical Interpretation* (Oxford, 1988); also G. B. Caird, ed. L. D. Hurst, *New Testament Theology* (Clarendon Press, 1994), and a review by the present author in the *Times Literary Supplement* (26 May 1995).

12 Though that does not mean that we are always aware of our own brands of 'falsification' as we give our own accounts of the same scriptures!

13 Cf., e.g., Polycarp, Luke and the Pastoral Epistles; see J. L. Houlden, *The Pastoral Epistles* (SCM, 1976, 1989), pp. 42f; S. G. Wilson, *Luke and the Pastoral Epistles* (SPCK, 1979).

14 J. L. Houlden (ed.) (SCM, 1995).

15 It is another matter how far this commendation has been embraced in other Vatican documents (or indeed those of other churches). It remains common for passages of Scripture to be adduced in support of statements arrived at by quite other means and to be used for their bare words, regardless of context. See in Houlden (ed.), op. cit., in n. 14, essays by Carroll and Houlden.

16 The idea that Scripture has multiple interpretations is, of course, long established, with roots in the early centuries, but those former distinctions, between the literal, moral and spiritual senses of the text, were very different from the range of questions which modern historical and literary enquiry have made available and even inevitable. See R. J. Coggins and J. L. Houlden (eds.), *A Dictionary of Biblical Interpretation* (SCM, 1990).

17 See F. Loofs, *Leitfaden sum Studium der Dogmengeschichte* (Max Niemeyer, 1950); J. L. Houlden, *Explorations in Theology* vol. 3 (SCM, 1978), ch. 2.

18 See, e.g., C. E. Gunton, *The Promise of Trinitarian Theology* (T. & T. Clark, 1991); *The One, the Three and the Many* (Cambridge, 1993).

19 For this piece of Tudor propaganda, see J. J. Scarisbrick, *Henry VIII* (Eyre and Spottiswoode, 1968), pp. 270ff.

20 For infallibility, see A. M. Farrer, *Interpretation and Belief* (SPCK, 1976), pp. 159ff; for eucharistic doctrine, see J. L. Houlden, *Connections* (SCM, 1986), p. 195, n. 32.

21 Not to mention the third reference point of creation itself, with the

whole having a recapitulatory character: Christ as new Adam and the End as Eden restored, with the Fall undone (1 Cor. 15:22; Rev. 22; Isa. 11:1–9; 65:17–25).

5 Christian Belief in Modern Britain: The Tradition Becomes Vicarious

Grace Davie

This chapter aims to construct a framework within which the maintenance of a Christian tradition in modern Britain can be better understood. A central aspect of this framework concerns the growing contradictions within the data which measure the multiple facets of religious life in this country. On the one hand, there is a cluster of variables concerned with feelings, experience and the more numinous religious beliefs; variables which demonstrate considerable – some would say remarkable – persistence not only in Britain, but in most of Western Europe. On the other, there is a set of variables which measure religious orthodoxy and regular participation, both of which reveal a demonstrable and much talked-about decline in almost all Western European countries.[1] It is, in my view, the mismatch between these two clusters which characterises the religious life of Britain in the last quarter of the twentieth century; a mismatch which is central to the understanding of religious tradition. It is, moreover, a situation which is nicely caught by the phrase 'believing without belonging', the theme of this chapter.[2]

But first two words of caution. The terms 'believing' and 'belonging' should not be considered too rigidly. The distinction between the two is intended to capture a mood, to suggest an area of enquiry, a way of looking at the problem, not to describe a detailed set of characteristics. Operationalising either or both of the variables too severely is bound to distort the picture. Both Hornsby-Smith (1992) and Short and Winter (1993) do this to some extent in their critique of 'belief without belonging'. But the question very quickly becomes semantic. It is clear that we need some way, if not this one, to describe the persistence of certain aspects of religiosity in British society despite the undeniable decline in church-going. A second point follows on. The relative persistence of belief (not necessarily Christian belief) in modern societies is neither good news nor bad news for the churches. It is, simply, a state of affairs that forms one part of the context in which the institutional representatives of Christianity find themselves; a factor that has to be taken into account if their ministry is to be in any way effective.

Bearing these remarks in mind, the chapter will start by presenting the British data which underpin the theme of 'believing without belonging'. It will then – in a second section – discuss a number of variations on this theme, notably the significance of both age and gender as crucial variables in the maintenance (or otherwise) of a Christian tradition. The third section interrogates the same issue from a more theoretical standpoint. It addresses two central questions: to what extent can a relatively small minority maintain a tradition on behalf of a non-practising but in the main believing majority; and, secondly, to what degree are the aspirations of the two groups in question – the belongers and the believers – consonant with one another? The implications of this discussion are crucial for a better understanding of the evolution of British religion. They are, in addition, of considerable significance for those who take responsibility for the future of the churches themselves.

The theme

In terms of religious practice and the 'harder' religious indicators, much of the material that follows is taken from figures published by the Christian Research Association, notably the latest editions of the *UK Christian Handbook*[3] and the variety of church censuses concerning British religious life which the Christian Research Association has produced through the 1980s and 1990s (see the Bibliography at the end of this chapter). For the earlier post-war decades, the Marc Europe statistics can be supplemented by data selected from *Churches and Churchgoers* by Currie, Gilbert and Horsley, from which a useful longer-term perspective can also be gleaned.

Table 1
Church Summary

			Church Members			
	1975	1980	1985	1990	1992	1994
Anglican	2,297,871	2,179,458	2,016,943	1,871,977	1,812,422	1,760,070
Baptist*	235,884	239,780	243,051	230,858	228,199	229,276
Roman Catholic	2,605,255	2,454,253	2,279,065	2,196,694	2,087,511	2,002,758
Independent*	240,200	227,782	225,634	221,444	214,246	219,200
Methodist*	576,791	520,557	474,290	443,323	434,606	420,836
New Churches*	12,060	25,250	80,494	125,869	149,558	164,317
Orthodox	196,850	200,165	223,721	265,968	276,080	283,897
Other Churches	137,083	131,510	126,127	121,681	120,609	119,453
Pentecostal*	101,648	126,343	136,582	158,505	169,071	183,109
Presbyterian	1,589,085	1,437,775	1,322,029	1,213,920	1,172,011	1,120,383
TOTAL	7,992,727	7,545,873	7,127,936	6,852,239	6,664,381	6,494,299
of which *Free Churches*	1,303,666	1,270,862	1,286,178	1,301,680	1,316,287	1,327,191
Percentage total as of adult population	18.5	16.9	15.5	14.7	14.3	13.9

* The six components of the Free Churches
  (Adapted from Brierley and Wraight, 1995:240.)

The data are unequivocal. Only 14 per cent of the population of Britain now claims membership of a Christian church in an active sense (Table 1), though the national variations masked by this overall percentage are considerable. There is, of course, some difficulty about the meaning of the term 'membership', for the term means different things for different people, an increasingly pertinent factor, given the growing pluralism of Britain's religious life. Membership should, moreover, be distinguished from practice; sometimes the two coincide but not necessarily so.[4] But these caveats aside, it remains abundantly clear that *both* church membership in an active sense *and* regular church attendance have become minority pursuits in contemporary Britain, and no amount of discussion regarding the niceties of the terminology used is able to disguise this fact. Nor is the situation likely to alter in the foreseeable future. Membership of the principal Christian denominations has declined sharply in the post-war period and continues to do so. The rate of decline is, however, uneven and some denominations have managed – temporarily at least – to arrest this trend altogether. So much so that some of the fall in membership in the mainline denominations has been offset by extremely rapid growth in a range of new churches, among Pentecostals and by a steady increase in the Orthodox population. These fast-growing congregations are, however, small; in consequence any changes in their numbers – though noticeable (sometimes extremely so) in percentage terms – make little impression on the membership statistics of the Christian churches taken as a whole. Two further points are worth noting within the overall percentages of the *active* Christian population: firstly, that the Roman Catholics have for some time outnumbered the Anglicans (so much for the significance of the Established Church in England), and secondly, that taken together the 'other Protestants' category (that is, the whole range of free churches together with the Presbyterians) have active membership figures which are higher than either the Roman Catholics or the Anglicans within the United Kingdom taken as a whole.

In terms of statistical patterns, the presence of other-faith communities in Britain is similar to the expanding Christian communities: the proportional growth is considerable but the overall figures remain small. There is, moreover, significant diversity within this category which needs constant recognition, for not all of the groups in question have expanded in the post-war period. The Jewish community, for example, used to be larger than it is. A further point is also important. The other-faith communities in Britain are noticeably more varied than their European counterparts in that Britain (or, to be more precise, England) now hosts a sizeable Sikh and Hindu population in addition to a significant Muslim presence. The members of all these communities come in the main from the Indian subcontinent;

Table 2
Religious Community

Total Religious Community in millions

	1975	1980	1985	1990	1992	1994	1995[1]
Anglicans[2]	28.2[3]	27.7[3]	27.1	26.6	26.4	26.2	26.1
Baptist[5]	0.6	0.6	0.6	0.6	0.6	0.6	0.6
Roman Catholic[2]	5.6[3]	5.7[3]	5.6	5.8	5.6	5.7	5.7
Independent[5]	0.5	0.5	0.5	0.4	0.4	0.4	0.4
Methodist	1.5	1.4	1.4	1.4	1.4	1.3	1.3
New Churches[5]	0.0	0.1	0.2	0.3	0.3	0.3	0.3
Orthodox	0.4	0.4	0.4	0.5	0.5	0.5	0.5
Other Churches[5]	0.3	0.3	0.3	0.2	0.2	0.2	0.2
Pentecostal[5]	0.2	0.3	0.3	0.3	0.3	0.4	0.4
Presbyterian[6]	2.9[3]	2.8[3]	2.7[3]	2.7[3]	2.7[3]	2.6	2.6
TOTAL Trinitarian Churches	40.2	39.8	39.1	38.6	38.4	38.2	38.1
Church of Scientology	0.1[3]	0.2[3]	0.3[3]	0.3[3]	0.3	0.4	0.5
Other non-Trinitarian Churches[5]	0.6[3]	0.6[3]	0.7[3]	0.8[3]	0.8[3]	0.8	0.8
Hindus	0.3[3]	0.4[3]	0.4[3]	0.4	0.4	0.4	0.4
Jews[6]	0.4	0.3[3]	0.3	0.3	0.3	0.3	0.3
Muslims	0.4[3]	0.6[3]	0.9[4]	1.0[3]	1.1	1.2	1.2
Sikhs[5]	0.2	0.3[3]	0.3[3]	0.5	0.5	0.5	0.6
Other religions	0.1	0.2	0.3	0.3	0.3	0.3	0.3
TOTAL non-Trinitarian and other Religions	2.1	2.6	3.2	3.6	3.7	3.9	4.1
TOTAL all religions	42.3	42.4	42.3	42.2	42.1	42.1	42.2
Percentage of population:							
Trinitarian Churches	72%[3]	71%[3]	69%[3]	67%[3]	66%	65%	65%
Non-Trinitarian churches and Other Religions	4%	5%	6%[3]	6%	6%	7%	7%
Total all religions	76%[3]	76%[3]	75%[3]	73%[3]	72%	72%	72%

[1] Estimate [2] Baptised membership [3] Revised figure [4] 852,900 more exactly [5] Taken as approximately double membership
[6] Based on the estimated baptised population in 1991 of 1.9 million for the Church of Scotland, the Northern Ireland 1991 Population Census, and twice the membership of all other Presbyterian Churches, giving a Community figure of 2.7 million in 1991.
(Adapted from Brierley and Wraight, 1995: 284.)

they reflect the nature of British imperial connections. Former imperial connections have also influenced the Christian presence in modern Britain. The Afro-Caribbean population arrived in this country for the same, largely economic reasons as the Asian communities. It is, however, a population of Christian origin and has led in recent decades to a number of thriving Afro-Caribbean congregations, some of the most lively amongst all the Christian churches of this country. These are communities which both believe and belong.

The figures for the other-faith populations are given in Table 2. Unlike the statistics so far discussed for the Christian churches of Britain, these figures concern community size rather than active religious membership. Turning now to the equivalent figures for the principal Christian groups in this country (the upper half of the same table), it is important to note a methodological shift. We are beginning to move to a rather different type of religious variable – that of nominal attachment rather than active participation. It is, moreover, at this point that the latent influence of the Church of England really begins to show; its nominal membership remains of a different order from that of any other denomination in this country. Nominal allegiance, moreover, is by no means the same as no allegiance at all. These categories have quite different implications, not only for the sociologist, but also for those responsible for pastoral care. And in Britain, nominal allegiance remains by far the most prevalent form of religious attachment; no allegiance is moderately rare, though less so than in many European countries.[5] The description of the Church of England as the church from which the English choose to stay away still – though for how much longer is difficult to say – catches the religious mood of a significant proportion of the English, if not the British population.

The situation can, perhaps, be summarised as follows: the considerable diversity both within the actively Christian communities and between a growing diversity of faiths (largely brought about by immigration) overlays a more or less Christian nominalism, symbolised in a passive attachment on the part of large numbers of the British population to their state churches. In England this nominalism takes Anglican forms; Presbyterianism, in the form of

97

the Church of Scotland, plays a similar role north of the border. In contrast, secularism – at least in any developed sense – remains the creed of a relatively small, though vocal, minority.

The distinction between nominalism and active religiosity can be reinforced if we turn now to patterns of religious belief in this country, in other words to believing rather than belonging. The evidence for some sort of religious belief is persuasive; it can be found in a wide variety of studies. A clutch of these took place in the early post-war decades. These are gathered together in chapter 3 of Martin's *Sociology of English Religion*, though reference to the originals, especially Gorer's studies and Mass Observation's *Puzzled People* will flesh out the bare bones of Martin's summary. On one point they all agree: in the early post-war decades, the British were by a considerable majority a believing people. Mass Observation (1948), for example, found that four out of five women and two out of three men 'give at least verbal assent to the possibility of there being a God, and most of the rest express doubt rather than disbelief. Uncompromising disbelievers in a Deity amount to one in twenty'.[6] The enquiries continued through a varied range of questions, revealing a high incidence of private prayer (though again not by any means related to church-going), much sympathy for religious education, a fair amount of antipathy towards organised religion and a truly wonderful confusion of doctrine. It is not difficult to see how elements of common religion antithetical to Christianity became incorporated into such beliefs, for it seems that orthodox Christian theology played a relatively small part in the everyday thinking of most British people.

How far do these results hold some 30 to 40 years later? Several enquiries came together in the 1980s and 1990s. One very detailed study took place in Leeds and involved some 1600 people, each of whom answered a lengthy questionnaire covering a wide variety of themes. A second was the European Values Study, first carried out in 1981 and repeated in 1990. The results of the 1981 and 1990 studies for a variety of religious indicators broadly confirm the findings of the Leeds investigation. For example, 71% of the sample report belief in God (76% in 1981); 54% (58% in 1981) define themselves as 'religious persons'; 53% (50%) regularly feel the need for prayer, meditation or contemplation; and 44% (46%) draw comfort or strength in religion. Conversely only 4.4% (4% in 1981) of the population emerge from the EVS data as convinced atheists. Such data can be correlated with a wide variety of socio-economic indicators. It is worth noting from the outset the significance of the age and gender variables within these correlations.

An additional British study took place in Islington in the late 1960s.[7] Though limited in scope and by now a little dated, the rigour with which this study was carried out has earned it a high reputation. It also includes one of the most revealing quotes of the literature. When respondents were probed about their belief in God, they were asked, 'Do you believe in a God who can change the course of events on earth?' To which one respondent replied, 'No, just the ordinary one.' Answers such as these point up the paradox at the heart of the whole question. What is the significance, sociological or otherwise, of an *ordinary* God? Is this, or is this not, evidence of religious belief? If it is not belief, what kind of categories are necessary to understand this persistent dimension of British (and indeed European) life, and how would these relate to more orthodox dimensions of religiosity? It is these questions that lie at the heart of a publication concerned with the evolution of a Christian tradition in this country. They are the obvious consequence of the detachment of belief from its moorings. No longer anchored by regular practice, belief drifts further and further away from anything that might be termed orthodoxy.

The conclusion of the Islington study is worth quoting at some length to illustrate this point. The citation provides, in addition, a number of clues towards understanding at least some of the processes involved:

> The analysis in the section above suggests the tentative conclusion that religious belief, when not associated with active

99

> membership of a church, tends to be associated with super-stitious belief while church attendance tends to be antithetical to superstition. Moreover, we have some evidence that for those people who do not go to church yet say they are religious and pray often, religious belief has moved quite far from the orthodox church position and is really much closer to what would normally be called superstition.[8]

Religious practice encourages the believer to resist elements antithetical to Christian doctrine. Given the marked decline in practice, such resistance is diminished. Belief, however, persists, increasingly 'contaminated' by elements incon-sistent with, even antithetical to, Christian teaching. This detachment of belief from regular practice is, in my view, a far greater challenge to the churches than the supposedly secular society in which we are thought to live. At the very least, it demands the sustained attention of scholars from a variety of disciplines.

Variations on the theme

There are any number of variations on the principal theme of this chapter. Broadly speaking, however, they can be grouped under four headings: national, regional, socio-logical and demographic. National differences reflect the markedly different religious cultures which make up the four countries of the United Kingdom. Regional differences reflect the considerable variety that can be found within the religious life of a moderately small nation (or combination of nations). Sociological differences concern the overlap between different parts of society (urban/ rural, affluent/ non-affluent etc.) and particular models of religious life. Finally, demographic variables reveal the very marked dif-ferences between men and women and between young and old in terms of their religious sensibilities. Each of these categories intersects with the others to produce a complex and constantly shifting kaleidoscope.[9]

In a publication such as this, the demographic differences are, I think, the most pertinent, for they demonstrate the crucial significance of generational change in the maintenance (or otherwise) of a religious tradition and the contrasting roles of men and women within these processes. The material on age and gender that follows summarises the fuller discussion in Davie (1994).

THE SIGNIFICANCE OF GENDER

Why is it that women are more religious than men; or to be more accurate, why are the religious sensitivities of women *different* from those of men? For not only does gender almost always appear as a significant variable, often *the* most significant, with respect to quantitative issues (how many individuals do or do not practise, do or do not believe), it is equally true that the nature – a more qualitative measure – of women's beliefs is different from those of their male counterparts. These differences hold throughout the age range.

The evidence is brought together very helpfully in a review of the literature published by Walter (1990)[10] in which he takes three dimensions of religiosity – churchgoing, private prayer and the content of religious belief – as a framework for further discussion. Each of these requires a little expansion. The disproportionate number of women going to church, for example, is amply confirmed by the figures from the 1989 Marc Europe census, from which an additional factor also emerges. Not only do the census figures underline the imbalance between the sexes, they indicate that this feature is becoming more rather than less marked in contemporary society.[11] In assessing such figures, however, it is important to keep in mind wider demographic shifts, particularly if the age variable is introduced as well. For church-going has, quite clearly, a particular appeal for a group that is prospering, demographically speaking, in modern Western society; that is, older women. The ratio of live females to live males increases with every step up the age scale, a difference that might account in part, though by no means entirely, for disproportionate numbers of women, especially in elderly congregations. A final point concerns denomination. Here the material is complex, but – once again – it is the mainline churches that demonstrate the greatest fall-off in attendance by men. The

101

independents, the Pentecostals and the Orthodox do better, if 'better' is an appropriate word in this context.

The mismatch between statistics relating to religious practice and those relating to religious belief provides the organising theme for this chapter. But quite apart from the discrepancy between belief and practice, *within* almost every question relating to religious belief there is a noticeable difference between the scores of men and women. For example, the Mori Poll carried out in 1989[12] – reinforcing the findings of the European Values Study already cited – discovered that 84% of the women in their sample believe in God, but only 67% of the men; in contrast only 9% of the women say that they do *not* believe in God as opposed to 16% of the men; 72% of the women believe in sin, 76% in a soul, 69% in heaven, 57% in life after death, 42% in the devil and 35% in hell. The corresponding figures for men were 66% (sin), 58% (a soul), 50% (heaven), 39% (life after death), 32% (the devil) and 27% (hell), differences that are very similar to those between the age groups (see below). Walter (following Argyle and Beit-Hallahmi, 1975) emphasises the dimension of private prayer as one where the contrasting behaviour of men and women is at its most marked,[13] prompting reflection about the relationship between the presence of men in religious activity and the extent to which this activity is designated either as public or private. If the private is beginning to predominate in some – though by no means all – aspects of contemporary religiosity, the significance of women as 'carriers' of that tradition may be increasing very rapidly indeed. Moreover, what they choose to carry may equally well be affected. For women, if they are asked to describe the God in whom they believe, concentrate rather more on the God of love, comfort and forgiveness than on the God of power, planning and control. Men, it seems, do the reverse. Interestingly, these contrasts show at a relatively early age, for they emerge in a number of studies of teenagers as well as in those using samples drawn from the adult population,[14] opening an inevitable but inconclusive debate about where such notions come from in the first place. Is it a question of nature or nurture?

102

This discussion leads into the second part of Walter's article, in which he begins to look for explanations: *why* are there such marked and consistent differences between men and women with respect to such a wide variety of religious indicators? The article collects together eleven social scientific theories grouped into three categories: the psychological theories (those which talk about guilt, anxiety and dependence and about God as the father figure); the deprivation–compensation theories (those concerning material poverty, status and the different opportunities that men and women have for social life); and, thirdly, a group of theories concerning the roles that women assume in society (including child-rearing, closely linked by Walter to sacrifice, the participation of women in the work-force and the privatisation of religion). Walter concludes, quite rightly, that it is most unlikely that any one of these 'theories' (and in many cases they are little more than suggestions) is likely to hold in every case. But taken together, and in flexible combinations, they may at least begin to indicate fruitful lines of research.

THE SIGNIFICANCE OF AGE

If we turn now to age, it is clear that older people have always been more religious than the young. Whether the elderly have regarded God as judgemental (the source of all their troubles) or as a father figure (a rock in the storm of life), they have always taken him more seriously than their sons and daughters. This kind of generational difference has been reflected in church membership studies for some time, and is, increasingly, supported by studies of religious belief. The Mori poll already quoted – once again reinforcing the European Values Study figures – illustrates this point clearly, revealing that 67% of those aged between 15 and 34 believe in God as against 87% of those aged over 55. Similarly, only 55% of the younger age group believe in heaven as opposed to 65% of the oldest. It seems that belief in God, and specifically belief in a personal God, declines with every step down the age scale, as indeed do practice, prayer and moral conservatism. In short, in Britain as in most of Western Europe, a religiously and morally conservative majority among the retired becomes a religiously conservative minority in the 18–24 age-group.

There is a crucial sociological question lurking in these data. Are we, in the late twentieth century, experiencing a marked *generational* shift with respect to religious behaviour, or are the variations so far indicated merely in accordance with the normal manifestations of the life cycle? *If* the former is the case – and the evidence is by no means conclusive – the implications for the future of religious life may be very considerable indeed. The point at issue forms a crucial thread within this chapter, which will be developed more fully in the following section. It can be summarised quite simply at this stage. How far can the familiar patterns of religious life maintain themselves if more and more people (among them increasing numbers of the young) opt out of active religiosity, not only temporarily but for the greater part of their lives? In other words, at what stage does the active and practising religious minority become so reduced that it ceases to have a realistic effect upon the host society?

One or two qualifications are, however, important before jumping to conclusions about possible future scenarios. The first concerns a shift that has already taken place in British society in the post-war period. It is, moreover, a shift that has been accommodated by the churches, though they may not always have been conscious of the change. *Pre-war* generations in Britain, to a greater extent than is often realised, grew up under the influence of the churches, or, at least, under the influence of a wide network of para-church organisations. By no means all British people practised their faith with regularity, but they possessed, nonetheless, a degree of religious knowledge that had some sort of connection with orthodox Christianity. This connection was most obviously expressed in the possession of a shared vocabulary; a common language which could be assumed, on either side, in encounters with the churches' personnel. Since the war, this pattern has altered radically, for it is the generation born immediately after the war that has, very largely, broken the formal link with the churches; hence the marked drop in both membership and attendance figures in the 1960s, when that generation came of age. But nominal belief in God persists, partly embodied in an accepting – and in some senses grateful – attitude to the churches, despite the lack of regular attendance. It is, however, a belief which is less and less influenced by Christian teaching, in the sense of shared knowledge and the means to express this. Orthodox Christianity and popular religion have, not surprisingly, been drifting further and further apart.

An inevitable corollary immediately suggests itself: is a further generational shift in religious behaviour upon us as the twentieth century draws to a close? In other words – following at least one line of evidence in the European Values Study – significant groups of young people (with all the provisos surrounding this problematic term) might be moving to the next stage: for them, in particular, disconnected belief is increasingly giving way to no belief at all, a conclusion for which there is a good deal of empirical support (notably in the work of Francis).[15] There is, however, another possibility. If the definition of religion is widened to include questions about individual and social health, about the purpose of existence, the future of the planet and the responsibilities of humanity both to fellow humans and to the earth itself, we may find a rather different pattern of 'religious' behaviour among the young. The evidence remains impressionistic, but it seems at least plausible that the younger age groups may respond to these profound ecological, moral, ethical (and, surely, religious) issues, much more constructively than they do to traditional religious beliefs. Indeed, their response may be considerably more positive than that of their elders.

A theoretical perspective

Imbalances between indices of belief or nominal attachment and those which measure religious orthodoxy and religious practice are often taken for granted, though why relatively high levels of belief and low levels of practice (rather than any other combination) should be considered 'normal' is far from clear. Nor is the persistence of some sort of belief

105

necessarily advantageous for the churches. All that can be said is that the relationship between belief and practice was different in the past and will, in all probability, be different again in the future. The analysis has to be repeated generation by generation. It is essential that the churches grasp the pressures of the late 1990s; operating a policy based on the assumptions of previous decades or conjectures about the future will only confuse the issue.

Bearing this in mind and building on to the reasoning so far presented, a whole set of sociological issues begin to assert themselves. They are best expressed as a series of questions. What, for example, is the nature of the relationship between the active religious minority on the one hand and the less active, but moderately believing majority on the other? How far is one dependent on the other and is the relationship between them likely to change in the foreseeable future? Does a believing majority make the work of the minority harder or easier? Do the former constitute a pool from which the latter can fish, or do they become, in part at least, a source of tension, a rival set-up, an alternative religious focus for society? If so, what is the nature of this alternative belief? Does this nature differ between men and women and between old people and young? Is there – to come back to the central argument of this chapter – a minimum size beyond which the active minority is no longer effective in society? What factors, apart from size, might determine this effectiveness? But questions, it seems, suggest themselves far more readily than answers. For in most cases we simply do not know what the relationship between religious practice and wider patterns of belief might be. I would like, nonetheless, to conclude by suggesting three areas of enquiry.[16] The common thread concerns the manner in which a relatively small minority might be able to influence the wider society.

THE INSTITUTIONAL CHURCHES

There can be no doubt at all that the institutional churches in Britain, as in most of Western Europe, have shrunk dramatically both in size and influence. No longer can they dominate major areas of policy; nor do they influence the moral decision-making, either public or private, of the majority within the population. Such churches remain, nonetheless, major actors on the stage of civil society, (an increasingly utilised term). Or to put the same point in a different way, churches have changed in nature during the course of the twentieth century. The 'sacred canopy' of earlier generations has given way to a series of voluntary associations (among them the Established Church), in which individuals participate in whatever manner suits them best. As voluntary associations, however, the churches are still remarkably effective. Political parties, trades unions and the sponsors of organised sport are envious – and rightly so – of the numbers involved in religious groups of the voluntary sector. They remain a major attraction for significant numbers of people in contemporary Britain. This is particularly true of women,[17] who not only appreciate the services of churches more readily than men, but are emerging more and more in positions of authority within them.

Built into the nature of the churches, however, is the care that they take of much wider sections of the population at certain points in their lives. Traditionally there have been three of these: birth, marriage and death. In Britain the contact with the Church when a new life begins has fallen sharply in the post-war period. Baptism figures in the Church of England, for example, have dropped from two-thirds of the population to one third since the 1950s. It is also the case that significant numbers of marriages now take place outside the churches' influence. Indeed, the pattern of marriage itself is changing rapidly in British society as the notion of marriage as a life-long partnership drifts away from the Christian norm. The same, however, cannot be said of ceremonies that take place at the moment of death. At this point if at no other, the churches come into contact with the vast majority of the British people. Such encounters have undoubtedly changed in the post-war period, for large numbers of these ceremonies (about 70%) now take place in the crematoria of modern Britain rather than the parish churches. It remains rare, however, that an individual life comes to an end without some marking of

107

the sacred, normally through the presence of an 'ordained' minister (more often than not an Anglican). It is a demanding and time-consuming aspect of ministry, without which British society would consider itself seriously impoverished.

The pastoral implications of this situation are immense. For example: if children and young people no longer grow up in the churches (from baptism onwards), how are enquiring adults to be made welcome at whatever time in life they may be prompted to make contact with a religious institution? How can such contacts be encouraged in a population which appears to maintain its religious sensitivities, but has lost the vocabulary through which to express them? Has liturgy any meaning for those whose lives have been lived beyond the influence of the institutional churches? Is an Established Church the most effective structure within which to nurture and encourage a more developed understanding of Christian teaching? Does it fit at all with the idea of a church as a voluntary organisation? Such tensions pervade parish life as the committed minority endeavour to balance their own enthusiasms with those of the surrounding community. It is realistic to assume that the pressures will become more rather than less acute as the present generation gives way to the next and the distance between belief and belonging increases correspondingly.

RELIGION AND EDUCATION

The debates concerning religious education in this country have to be seen in an historical perspective. Like some, but unlike other European countries, there has in Britain been no major rupture between Church and State. One consequence of this situation is the sizeable sector of the educational service still dominated by the churches.[18] Denominational schools, particularly Church of England and Roman Catholic establishments, play a significant part in publicly funded educational provision. They are, moreover, extremely popular schools, often heavily oversubscribed. Given such a situation, those who make the decisions concerning entry to such schools face difficult

108

decisions. Should entry be limited to the church-going constituency or should it be extended as far as possible into the population? Different schools come to different conclusions. A further paradox can be widely documented: the fact that families with children of the appropriate age *become* church-goers, at least temporarily, in order to acquire the necessary accreditation for entry into the denominational school of their choice. They do not, for the most part, do this for religious reasons. They are, rather, attracted to such schools for their relatively good examination results and for the emphasis that many of them place on pastoral care. In order to achieve such goals, the 'religious' dimension of such schools is tolerated by a section of the population otherwise unattraced by religion.

Religious education in the classroom raises rather different issues, and here a very marked shift has taken place in the post-war period. The change can be exemplified with reference to two major pieces of educational legislation: the Butler Act of 1944 and the Baker Act of 1988. Each of these reflects the religious situation prevalent at that time. In 1944, for example, an Agreed Syllabus of Religious Instruction was established; this was a non-denominational form of teaching just about acceptable to Anglicans and Nonconformists,[19] but with no anticipation that the situation might change. In other words, with no anticipation that within 20 years there might be significant other-faith communities in many British cities. The 1988 Act had to confront this issue. It did so in a manner that displays a noticeable degree of defensiveness. The shifting religious environment was indeed acknowledged, but the 'broad traditions of Christian belief' must be upheld. These were underpinned in the Act by clauses which prescribed the amounts of time to be given to different faiths in the syllabi recommended. It *is* possible for some schools to offer a syllabus more closely related to the population within the school, but only by contracting out of what is considered normative. The same insistence on a Christian tradition can be found in the parts of the Act that deal with religious worship in state schools.

Prescription in religious education is one thing, practice quite another. The real problem resides in who exactly is going to carry out this very difficult task. In other words, is it possible to find sufficient teachers of high quality who can both instruct young people about religions (Christian and other), but allow them to make up their own minds about complex and difficult issues, including their own commitment or resistance to faith? On present showing, such teachers are very rare, but they do exist. There can be little doubt that they are key figures in the transmission of religious culture in British society.[20] Religious *knowledge* – such as it is – amongst young people is far more likely to come from the educational system than from the institutional churches.

RELIGIOUS BROADCASTING

In many ways, religious broadcasting takes believing without belonging to its logical conclusion, for it permits – even encourages – a rather self-indulgent form of armchair religiosity. It remains, moreover, a relatively popular activity in modern Britain.[21] Religious broadcasting needs, however, to be set in context, for like any other form of broadcasting, it reflects the wider nature of an advanced industrial society. A form of society, that is, where the small screen competes (often with overwhelming success) with the equivalent activity in 'real life', whether this be in politics, in sport, in leisure activities or in religion itself. It is society that is changing rather than the nature of religiosity. Such success creates, nonetheless, a situation of ambivalence for the churches. On the one hand, local congregations lose out to the professionalism of skilled religious broadcasters. There can be no doubt about this. But the churches know perfectly well that this same professionalism makes good a number of their own deficiencies. At the very least, the broadcasters bolster the values in society on which both they and the churches depend for survival. They can also make an impact in parts of society beyond the reach of the institutional churches.

A second factor needs, however, to be taken into account. The nature of broadcasting itself is altering, and so rapidly that it is hard to keep track. There are two interrelated aspects to this question. Firstly a technological one: new outlets, new skills and new possibilities are emerging all the time. Alongside this the legal or regulatory framework is also shifting, partly in response to the technological development. Deregulation is inevitable, for once one outlet is controlled, another will emerge to replace it. Effective authority becomes more and more difficult. An obvious set of sociological questions follow concerning who, exactly, will have access to this crucially significant medium and on what terms? Will the religious broadcasters, for example, be able to compete at all with other forms of 'entertainment'? Or will they simply be swept away in favour of others with higher audience figures? But always assuming that survival is possible, a second issue is bound to present itself. Which groups *within* the religious sector will be able to operate most effectively in a highly competitive market-place and which will fall by the wayside? British resistance to American-style televangelism dominates the current debate concerning religious broadcasting; whether it will withstand the force of the market in the longer term remains to be seen.

So much for the buying of media time. Equally significant are questions about the effect of the media on the messages transmitted, for handing on the faith by means of the small screen (or whatever comes next as a principal source of communication) will have consequences quite different from those that result from weekly encounters with the churches' personnel within designated sacred places. Obligation gives way to consumption. In the British case, the result is somewhat paradoxical, for the most popular form of religious broadcast in this country embodies a deeply traditional form of religion. Programmes which draw on hymn-singing and the community culture that goes with it continue to command large audiences on both radio and television, particularly among elderly people. The debate, however, needs to be set within a wider discussion of religious transmission which takes into account the changing capacities of the audience. Younger generations, for example, have never learnt the hymns in the first place; they are unlikely to respond either now or in later life to their electronic endorsement.

111

Conclusion: a note on doubting bishops

In many ways the framework of this chapter reflects a situation recognisable in the previous one, namely that familiarity with the patristic tradition is now the preserve of a small minority of academic scholars, not the common currency of those with a classical education. A similar shift can be seen in the knowledge base of modern society. To assume even the most basic Christian knowledge in most of Britain in the last decade of the twentieth century would be a mistake; such information is now the preserve of a relatively small minority, not of the population as a whole. Within the framework of this chapter, a second question follows on. Do the conditions of modern Britain (not least a widespread tendency to believe something) enable or disable the active Christian minority from operating, if not always effectively, then at least vicariously? In other words, is it possible for a relatively small group of people to maintain a Christian tradition on behalf of a much larger number, characterised – it seems – by indifference rather than hostility?

Evidence that this might be so can be found in a recent episode concerning the General Synod. In February 1996, a report was published[22] which contained entirely predictable material about the nature of the Synod. It incorporated a short section on the responses of members (including the House of Bishops) to a number of contemporary issues. The press coverage was immediate and extraordinary: it took the form of yet another instance of 'doubting bishops'. The tabloid papers *expect* the bishops to maintain the credal statements of Christian teaching; they are severe, to say the least, towards those who fail – or who are thought to fail – in this task. Every other page of the tabloid press indicates, however, that the implications of credal beliefs are ignored by 90% of their readership for 90% of the time. Hence the paradox of modern British society. We may indeed have relegated religious activity to the margins of social life, we may indeed disregard the precepts of Christian teaching for the greater part of our lives, but we still require them to be there. If those who are appointed to 'look after' the faith let us down, we become inordinately angry.

Such a situation can be variously interpreted. From a positive point of view, it encourages the conclusion that not only can a Christian tradition be maintained in modern British society, but also it is in fact welcomed by a surprisingly large number of people. There is, however, another rather more negative reading of the data. Is the 'tradition' so frequently demanded by the tabloids the living tradition of Christian teaching, or is it simply a legitimation of nostalgia that evokes a society which never really existed in the first place? The response to the survey – as indeed to other instances of 'doubting bishops' – indicates the latter just as much as the former. Creative thinking isn't welcome in a society that looks backwards rather than forwards. The bishops are hemmed in by expectations that they cannot possibly fulfil. How, then, can they maintain a living, vital tradition in the conditions of modern British society? First and foremost by recognising the *specificity* of the tensions that present themselves in the late 1990s. Out-of-date assumptions, whether these be positive (an informed Christian culture) or negative (developed secular opposition), must be left behind.

Notes to Chapter 5

1 There are, of course, exceptions to this pattern in Western Europe, notably the two parts of Ireland, both North and South.
2 The phrase 'believing without belonging' was first coined in a presentation to the 1989 Conference of the International Society for the Sociology of Religion. The paper was later published in *Social Compass* (1990b, vol. 37). For subsequent developments of this theme, see Davie, 1990a, 1993 and 1994.
3 Brierley and Longley, 1991; Brierley and Hiscock, 1993; Brierley and Wraight, 1995.
4 Brierley, 1991a: 56–7.
5 The number of British people expressing no allegiance grew dramatically between the 1981 and 1990 European Values Studies. The 1990 figure of 42% surprised everyone, but should probably be treated with caution.
6 1948: 156.

7 Abercrombie *et al.*, 1970.

8 Ibid.: 124.

9 See Davie, 1994: chs. 7 and 8 for a full discussion of these patterns.

10 Further reviews are shortly to appear; see the series of articles published in a special issue of *Archives de Sciences Sociales des Religions*, 1996, 94/3 and Davie and Walter (forthcoming).

11 For example: 'In 1979 the proportion of male churchgoers was 45%. In 1989 in England it had dropped to 42%, nearer to the 1982 Welsh figure of 38% and the 1984 Scottish figure of 37% . . . two-thirds of the change in church-going in the last decade reflects a fall-off by males' (Brierley, 1991b: 79).

12 Jacobs and Worcester, 1990.

13 This point is strongly supported by recent data from Switzerland.

14 In, for example, Martin and Pluck (1977) and Argyle and Beit-Hallahmi (1975: chs. 4 and 5).

15 The work of Leslie Francis in this area is very extensive. A useful summary can be found in Hyde (1990). Much of Francis' work is published in the *British Journal for Religious Education*.

16 There are, of course, other possibilities. The moral framework within which questions of law and ethics are considered is one of these. The traditional frameworks, largely derivative of Christian teaching, are crumbling, but no alternatives have emerged to replace them. The churches are still required to make a contribution in this area, despite their minority position.

17 The situation of the churches in modern Britian is often constructed with negative overtones: 'However almost any other activity that attracted the committed involvement of up to a tenth of the population, the passive sympathy of two-thirds to four-fifths of a sample, and was only rejected by one-twentieth of respondents, would be regarded as a successful and influential historical force' (Wolffe, 1994: 428). It is important not to forget the alternative persective.

18 At this point it is important to note that Scotland has a different educational system from the rest of the country. It is a system of which the Scottish are justly proud. For England, precise and up-to-date figures of the voluntary sector are available from Culham College Institute. In February 1993, 23.6% of all *pupils* were being educated in the voluntary sector, which was responsible for 32.1% of all publicly maintained *schools*.

19 The Catholics had their own syllabus in 1944. Fifty years later, religious education in Catholic schools remains a rather different activity from that in other schools (whether these be Anglican or state schools). Catholics continue to teach the Catholic faith in the sense of handing on a particular tradition. This is no longer the case in most schools, including Anglican ones. The understanding that Catholic schools exist primarily for Catholic children remains strong.

20 It is worth underlining that teachers of religious education in this country form part of the professional teaching community. They are not sponsored by any particular denomination.

114

21 Svennevig *et al.*, 1988.
22 Davie and Short, 1996.

Bibliography

Much of this chapter summarises the arguments of G. Davie, *Religion in Britain since 1945: Believing without Belonging* (Oxford, Blackwell, 1994). That in turn draws heavily on the figures produced by the Christian Research Association (formerly Marc Europe). These are listed in the references under Brierley, P. and his associates. These publications fall into two groups: first the series of *UK Christian Handbooks* (new editions appear every two years); secondly the series of church censuses carried out in England (1980, 1983 and 1990), Wales (1983) and Scotland (1984 and 1995). Tables 1, 2 and 3 are based on Christian Research Association figures, whose help is gratefully acknowledged. Comparative figures can be taken from the European Values Study (see Abrams *et al.*, 1985).

Abercrombie, N., Baker, J., Brett, S. and Foster, J., 'Superstition and religion: the God of the gaps', in Martin, D. and Hill, M. (eds.), *A Sociological Yearbook of Religion in Britain*, vol. 3, London, SCM, 1970, pp. 91–129.

Abrams, M., Gerard, D. and Timms, N. (eds.), *Values and Social Change in Britain*, London, MacMillan, 1985.

Argyle, M. and Beit-Hallahmi, B., *The Social Psychology of Religion*, London, Routledge, 1975.

Brierley, P. (ed.), *Prospects for the Eighties*, vols. 1 and 2, London, Marc Europe, 1980 and 1983.

—— *The UK Christian Handbook 1983 edition*, London, Marc Europe, 1982.

—— *Christian England*, London, Marc Europe, 1991a.

—— *Prospects for the Nineties* (11 vols.), London, Marc Europe, 1991b.

Brierley, P. and Hiscock, V. (eds.), *The UK Christian Handbook 1994/95 edition*, London, Christian Research Association, 1993.

Brierley, P. and Longley, D. (eds.), *The UK Christian Handbook 1992/93 edition*, London, Marc Europe, 1991.

Brierley, P. and Wraight, H. (eds.), *The UK Christian Handbook 1996/97 edition*, London, Christian Research Association, 1995.

Currie, R., Gilbert, A. and Horsley, L., *Churches and Churchgoers*, Oxford, Clarendon Press, 1977.

Davie, G., ' "An Ordinary God": the paradox of religion in contemporary Britain', in *British Journal of Sociology*, vol. 41, 1990a, pp. 395–421.

—— 'Believing without Belonging: Is this the future of religion in Britain?', in *Social Compass*, vol. 37, 1990b, pp. 456–69.

'Believing without belonging: a Liverpool case study', in *Archives de Sciences Sociales des Religions*, vol. 81, 1993, pp. 79–89.

—— *Religion in Britain since 1945: Believing without Belonging*, Oxford, Blackwell, 1994.

Davie, G. and Short, C., *Church of England General Synod 1990–1995: an analysis of membership*, London, Church House Publishing, 1996.

Davie, G. and Walter, T., 'The Religiosity of Women: understanding a paradox', forthcoming (typescript available from the authors).

Gorer, G., *Exploring English Character*, London, Cresset Press, 1955.

—— *Death, Grief and Mourning in contemporary Britain*, London, Cresset Press, 1965.

Gunter, B. and Viney, R., *Seeing is believing: religion and television in the 1990s*, London, John Libbey/IBA, 1994.

Hornsby-Smith, M., 'Believing without belonging? The case of Roman Catholics in England', in Wilson, B. (ed.), *Religion: contemporary issues*, London, Bellew Publishing, 1992, pp. 125–34.

Hyde, K., *Religion in Childhood and Adolescence: a comprehensive review of research*, Alabama, Religious Education Press, 1990.

Jacobs, E. and Worcester, R., *We British: Britain under the MORI-scope*, London, Weidenfeld and Nicholson, 1990.

Martin, D., *A Sociology of English Religion*, London, Heinemann, 1967.

—— *A General Theory of Secularization*, London, Blackwell, 1978.

Martin, B. and Pluck, R., *Young People's Beliefs*, A report to the Board of Education of the Church of England, 1977.

Mass Observation, *Puzzled People; a study of popular attitudes to religion, ethics, progress and politics in a London borough*, London, Victor Gollancz, 1948.

Short, C. and Winter, M., 'Believing and Belonging: religion in rural England', in *British Journal of Sociology*, vol. 44, 1993, pp. 635–51.

Svennevig, M., Haldane, L., Spiers, S., and Gunter, B., *Godwatching: Viewers, religion and television*, London, John Libbey/IBA, 1988.

Wallis, R. and Bruce, S., *Sociological Theory, Religion and Collective Action*, Belfast, Queen's University, 1986.

Walter, A., 'Why are most churchgoers women?', in *Vox Evangelica*, vol. 20, 1990, pp. 73–90.

Wolffe, J., 'Religion and "secularization" ', in Johnson, P. (ed.), *Twentieth Century Britain: economic, social and cultural change*, London, Longman, 1994, pp. 427–41.

6 Life in the Spirit: Contemporary and Christian Understandings of the Human Person

Linda Woodhead

Our view of the tradition should not be determined by what the previous generation said and did

When 'Christianity' and 'the Christian tradition' come under attack it often seems that what detractors have in their targets is not two thousand years of Christian history, but the Christianity of their youth and of the previous generation. I have a hunch therefore that the sharply hostile reaction to 'traditional Christianity' which was such a feature of the 1960s, and which continues in the writings of those influenced by that era, often has its roots not in a considered response to the Christian tradition in its fullness, but in an impatience with the failings of the immediate pre- and post-war period.

In preparation for writing this chapter on Christian anthropology (i.e. the investigation of what it is to be human) I read its equivalent in *Soundings* (1962), a chapter by Harry Williams entitled 'Theology and Self-Awareness'. My hunch was borne out by this chapter, which commends Freud's insights and suggests that they must transform Christianity. But reading Williams' telling criticisms of Christianity here and elsewhere, one gets the clear impression that what he is attacking is not so much the Christian heritage, but Anglican Christianity of the inter-war and immediate post-war periods, a Christianity which he sees as in denial, as prudish, priggish, obsessed with respectability and status, and by a refusal to face up to the realities of its day (a picture confirmed by Monica Furlong in her recent autobiography, *Bird of Paradise*).

What I wish to suggest in this chapter is that 'Christianity' or 'the Christian tradition' is far richer and more varied than that which a previous generation made of it (by tradition I mean something very inclusive: what has been said and done and made throughout Christian history, the Bible included). As such, tradition offers us a unique gift: the ability to transcend to some extent the contingencies of our times and to realise that where we are now is not the only place to be. I hope to play out these themes in relation to the same topic which Harry Williams addressed: Christian anthropology. Many charges are currently made against Christian thought about what it is to be human: that it is destructively dualistic and body-denying, that it is bleakly negative in its understanding of the human as sinner, that it postulates a distant, transcendent God who has no real contact with human beings. By taking the Christian tradition to be something wider than the Christianity of a previous generation, I hope to show that these charges have shakier foundations than is usually imagined.

Because this is a short chapter, I have to be selective in the elements of tradition I consider. I have therefore chosen to focus primarily upon the Bible – and especially Paul's letters – and also to make passing mention of elements of Augustine's thought about the human. I have made this selection not only because of the constitutive importance of these elements of the tradition for later Christianity, but because they are often singled out for attack as responsible for many of the worst faults of a Christian anthropology. What I hope to show is that they are being made to carry the sins of the previous generation, but that if allowed to speak with their own voice we may find that they have in fact much to teach us about what it is to be human, and that this may be deeply challenging to the alternative pictures of what it is to be human which have become influential in recent times. In particular I shall contrast the Christian anthropology which emerges from this traditional investi-

119

gation with what I refer to as an 'anthropology of the spiritual self', a popular understanding of the human which has captured the imagination of many people today, both inside and outside the churches.

An anthropology of the spiritual self and its growing influence

In its insistence upon the priority of the self and self-awareness in the religious life, Harry Williams' *Soundings* chapter sounds one of the major themes of much contemporary anthropological thought. It is a theme which is foundational for the contemporary anthropology I wish to discuss in this chapter, the anthropology of the spiritual self. Williams himself does not develop such an anthropology in its fullness, and he would certainly have been wary of many of its teachings. But many Christians who have followed Williams in the liberal tradition have moved further than he, and have endorsed some version of an anthropology of the spiritual self. Nor have they been alone in doing so. For many outside the churches as well as within them have developed such an anthropology, particularly those who are interested in 'alternative' forms of spirituality. An anthropology of the spiritual self lies at the very heart of the New Age movement, for example.[1] It is, in short, a way of thinking about what it is to be human which attracts many people of the late twentieth century who have a spiritual bent, both Christian and post-Christian.

An anthropology of the spiritual self so emphasises the centrality of the self and the importance of self-awareness that it construes the spiritual quest in terms of 'self-realisation'. It teaches that knowledge of self and love of self are preconditions of a healthy relationship with God and others. Self must come first. Correspondingly, anthropology – the science of the self and its development – must become what Levinas would call 'first science', the foundation of all other disciplines. And consequently, an anthropology of the spiritual self is more than a mere anthropology, it is an entire world-view, ethic and spirituality; for the self is given epistemological, ontological and ethical primacy. By explaining each of these primacies in turn it is possible to build up a sketch of this anthropology which can be further fleshed out in what follows.

First, the self has epistemological primacy. An anthology of the spiritual self assumes that all thought is reducible to 'experience' – something which is directly present within an individual's consciousness and never fully communicable to another person. Everything, including religious experience and dogma is thought to boil down to such experience. The experience of individuals with unique spiritual insight (like Buddha and Christ) is said to form the basis of the great religions, but a basis which does not obviate the need for each subsequent individual to have his or her own spiritual experience. Thus the quest for God is identified with the individual's quest for religious experience. God is what we construct on the basis of such experience, indeed in an important sense God *is* that experience. God may be immediately present to consciousness. Revelation is a spiritual experience, an 'expansion of consciousness'. By contrast, religion without experience is said to be dry, dull and second-hand: 'mere faith'. Experience must always be the judge of religion and religious tradition.[2]

Second, the self has ontological primacy. For an anthropology of the spiritual self, the self is thought to be the most real reality – indeed, the only true reality.[3] This conclusion about the ontological priority of the self is closely tied up with belief in the epistemological priority of the self. As we have seen, this anthropology claims not just that the divine may be known by consciousness, but that in an important sense the divine *is* consciousness – and, conversely, consciousness is the divine. In a true 'expansion of consciousness' enlightened people do not just know the divine, they realise that they are one with the divine. They realise that the mind which is in them is one with the divine mind, that there is no subject–object duality but a spiritual unity. Thus mind or consciousness is identified as the truly real part of me, of the world, and of all reality. Often it is referred to as 'Spirit', that which underlies all things and of which all things are manifestations.

Third, the self has ethical primacy. The reason for this

121

should by now be clear. Since all things and all people are manifestations of Spirit, by realising my true spiritual self, I realise my unity with all things. I know that I am Spirit, the same Spirit that is in all things. Self-knowledge thus inevitably results in a sense of my 'connectedness' with everything. This is the basic ethical sensibility. It will ensure that I act with love, respect and tenderness towards all living and non-living things. As the feminist theologian Mary Grey puts it, 'Re-connecting – earlier I called this "redeeming connections" – claims to be *divine*, because it is re-rooting in the basic relational energy of the universe.'[4]

An anthropology of the spiritual self has been growing in influence throughout the course of this century. It is stated over and over again in remarkably similar terms in almost all the literature associated with the New Age movement. It appears with the same consistency in much of the spiritual literature which has been influenced by the ecological movement, including eco-feminism. It also appears within much popular spiritual literature, in the discussion of spiritual matters in glossy magazines, in many self-help manuals – and even within some new managerial theory and training methods.[5] And it appears increasingly influential within Christianity itself. Even within academic theology, versions of an anthropology of the spiritual self now appear with increasing frequency, particularly within works of radical theology. So, for example, much feminist theology propounds an anthropology of the spiritual self,[6] as does much green theology, including Matthew Fox's Creation Theology.[7] Interestingly, it was Fox's ideas which influenced the 'Planetary Mass' at the Nine O'clock Service in Sheffield recently; it is surely a measure of the growing influence of an anthropology of the spiritual self that this development was welcomed even by the hierarchy of the Church of England.

Aspects of anthropology in the Christian tradition contrasted with an anthropology of the spiritual self

Although many Christians now seem to believe that an anthropology of the spiritual self enshrines properly

122

Christian insights about the human person, I wish to suggest that a serious engagement with aspects of traditional Christian thought about the person suggests the opposite. For such an engagement reveals important differences and incompatibilities between the two anthropologies. Here I will mention a few of the most important.

In the first place, anthropology is *not* first science for Christianity. It is not one of the traditional topics of Christian reflection or credal confession. That is not to say that Christianity is uninterested in the human person, but that it believes we cannot understand the human by beginning with the human. This difference of perspective is interestingly revealed in the different vocabularies and conceptualities which the two anthropologies employ. Whereas an anthropology of the spiritual self speaks of 'self', Christian texts tend to use words equivalent to the English 'Man', 'person', 'human being', or 'creature'. The language instantiates the fact that whereas an anthropology of the spiritual self views the human being from a first-person perspective, Christianity typically adopts a third-person perspective. And this perspective is not just that of other humans, it is that of God.

Thus Christianity, unlike an anthropology of the spiritual self, tends to view human beings in *relational* terms. To speak of a human 'creature', for example, is to speak of a being who exists in relation to the Creator God, and in a relation of likeness with the rest of the created order. And to speak of a 'human' or a 'person' is similarly to speak of a being who is related to the Creator and the rest of creation in a certain way. As the Genesis 1 and Psalm 8 explain, 'Man' is that creature who is situated between God and the animals and plants:

> thou hast made him little less than God,
> and dost crown him with glory and honour.
> Thou hast given him dominion over the works of thy hands;
> thou hast put all things under his feet.

For biblical and Christian thought, what it is to be human, to be a creature, is not to exist as an autonomous individual

123

substance, but to be related in certain given ways to God, to fellow human beings, and to the rest of the created order.

Christianity's relational perspective on the human frees it from the necessity of speculation about human substance. By contrast, an anthropology of the spiritual self is greatly exercised by this matter. Its understanding of the human is not primarily relational but substantive: the human is the *spiritual* self. Compared with this, the Bible has a very untidy metaphysic of the human. The Bible speaks of body, flesh, mind, soul and spirit, but without ever clearly defining or demarcating the terms in relation to the human. Even more confusing to an anthropology of the spiritual self, the Bible seems to blur the categories of body and mind. The two are rarely contrasted clearly and are rarely viewed as either distinct or separable. So, for example, both Old and New Testaments witness to a belief that soul and body die together – suggesting that the soul is not viewed as infinite, eternal nor separable from body. So, similarly, the New Testament understands the afterlife in terms of resurrection rather than the immortality of a soul freed from the body. And so too both Old and New Testaments often speak of the essence of each human being as 'the heart', something which cannot be neatly characterised either as spiritual or bodily, but hovers ambiguously between them.

Of all the books in the Bible, those by the apostle Paul may seem at first glance to give most encouragement to a metaphysic of human substance like that of the spiritual self, for Paul at least draws a clear distinction between 'flesh' (*sarx*) and 'spirit' (*pneuma*). Yet a closer look shows that Paul is just as confused (by the lights of an anthropology of the spiritual self) as other biblical writers, for his *sarx* and his *pneuma* do not in fact correspond to the 'body' and 'mind/spirit' of an anthropology of the spiritual self. Instead of using the contrasting pair *sarx* and *pneuma* in a substantial sense, Paul uses them in a relational one. He uses them to speak of a human being's relation to God and neighbour: those who are incorporate in Jesus Christ have become new *spiritual* creatures, and have put off their old *fleshly* lives. But as far as human substance is concerned,

124

Paul has little to say. In general he seems to view human beings as an inseparable unity of body and soul (*psyche*) or mind (*nous*); but this is a matter of altogether less importance to him than the fact that this human unity – body and soul – may be either 'fleshly' or 'spiritual'. It is this way of thinking which enables him to form that conception so unthinkable in the terms of an anthropology of the spiritual self (or Platonism): the 'spiritual body' (*sōma pneumatikon*) of the resurrection (1 Cor. 15:44). For Paul, to be a Christian is to have both soul and body transformed by Spirit.

It is this very biblical way of thinking which imbues Paul's thought about the things of the Spirit with such an earthy or materialist flavour. So, for example, he can equate the gift of the Spirit with *incorporation* into the *body* of Christ, thinking of this union in quasi-physical terms and even likening it to the sexual union of husband and wife (Eph. 5:22–33; cf. 1 Cor. 6:15–20). As he says of the Church's relation to Christ: 'we are members of his body, of his flesh, and of his bones' (Eph. 5:30). Likewise, Paul has no difficulty in accepting that the gift of the Spirit may be given in the gifts of bread, wine and water, and in mixing up Platonic categories by saying, for example, '[we] have all been made to drink into one Spirit' (1 Cor. 12:13). Paul's thought is not inhibited by the blockage which a neat Platonic distinction between body and mind, material and spiritual has bequeathed to the modern world, a blockage which allows only matters of the spirit, quite separate from matters bodily and material, to pass through into the realm of religion. And it is surely this very blockage, reinforced by the rise of natural science, which has given rise to the idea of the spiritual self, an idea far removed from the Christian tradition of thought about the human which takes its rise from the Bible.

An anthropology of the spiritual self emerges as more strongly dualistic than a Christian anthropology

The Christian understanding of the human person is often accused of being dualistic – not least by an anthropology of the spiritual self. Yet even the brief comments I have made

125

above suggest that this conclusion receives no support from biblical thought about the human. Besides the Bible, Augustine is often cited as guilty in this matter. But here again the realities of the tradition confound the criticisms levelled against it: especially if what is to count as a destructive dualism is spelt out clearly.

In recent times 'dualism' seems to have become a blanket term of abuse. This is a little thoughtless, for there are surely good and helpful dualisms as well as bad and destructive ones – even in anthropology. Here the dualism which many Christian thinkers display seems not just benign, but quite helpful in making sense of the human condition. This is a dualism which distinguishes between the realities of mind/soul and body, and which sometimes goes on to assert that the mind/soul should rule the body. But to accept that mind/soul and body are thus distinguishable is quite different from accepting that they are either separable or opposed to one another. In these strong and destructive senses, neither the Bible nor the overwhelming proportion of pre-modern Christianity is dualistic. And even those thinkers who imagine the mind and body to be temporarily separable (imagining, for example, a disembodied state between death and resurrection) hope for a final consummation in which renewed soul and body will be permanently reunited.

All this is as true of Augustine as of other Christian thinkers. Certainly Augustine believes that it is possible to distinguish soul and body, and certainly he believes that the former should control the latter. But he regards the perfect human being as one in which soul and body are united in perfect harmony.[8] In speaking of their separation into two opposed principles he is not outlining an ontology, but describing the results of the Fall. For Augustine, the unity of soul and body is given by God in creation, and perfected in redemption (resurrection). Both soul and body participate in the history of redemption, and the body is by no means excluded from it.[9] Augustine considers the nature of the resurrection body and its physical perfections in great detail, considering what height the body will have, what age it will be, what sex, what weight, and even what will

126

happen to amputated parts.[10] And he is at great pains throughout all discussions about the resurrection body to insist that Paul's comment that it will be a 'spiritual body' does not mean it is made of spiritual rather than material substance, but that it will be wholly animated by the Holy Spirit and made incorruptible.

Attention to those aspects of the Christian tradition most commonly accused of being destructively dualistic in their attitude towards the human thus gives the lie to the charge. Indeed, comparison of these aspects of the tradition with an anthropology of the spiritual self suggests a paradoxical conclusion: that it is in fact the latter which is more guilty of destructive dualism. For although an anthropology of the spiritual self claims to be holistic and completely opposed to all forms of dualism, the truth seems a little different. This anthropology is not so much holistic as monistic, for it reduces all reality to one principle: Spirit. And, as we have seen, it identifies Spirit with mind or consciousness. In making this move, it implicitly draws a distinction between spirit/mind and body (that which is not mind). So its assertion that all is Spirit forces it to view the material and the bodily as ultimately illusory. Matter/the body is viewed as a benign manifestation of Spirit, but nevertheless as a manifestation which is merely temporary and fleeting: ultimately an illusion. Matter is a manifestation in which Spirit travels the furthest from its true self, taking a form which is least transparent to its true spiritual reality and so capable of misinterpretation as a separate reality.[11] For an anthropology of the spiritual self, then, what is ultimately real in a person is not body but consciousness. And this, surely, is a much stronger dualism than anything found in Christianity, a destructive dualism which cannot accept that the human is now and in the next life a differentiated reality of mind and matter, body and soul. Rather, an anthropology of the spiritual self de-sacralises the body and removes it from the economy of salvation.

This implicit dualism of an anthropology of the spiritual self was captured in a slogan which emerged in some of its early forms: 'mind over matter'.[12] Some of the most influential early forms of the anthropology applied this slogan

127

directly in techniques of healing, thus giving rise to forms of 'alternative medicine' which viewed disease as spiritual in origin, and which sought cures by means of a change in mental attitude rather than by physical intervention.[13] Such traditions of healing have proliferated during the last few decades. Like the anthropology of the spiritual self with which they are so closely linked, they claim to be 'holistic', and do indeed take the body very seriously. Yet their implicit dualism is evident in the way they nevertheless view the body as under the complete control of the mind, and ultimately as reducible to Spirit. As a result they view so-called physical disease as curable by the mind, by 'positive thinking'. As the body has no separate reality from the mind, bodily disorder must be put right by spiritual practice.

Equally revealing of the implicit dualism of an anthropology of the spiritual self are its attitudes towards death and the afterlife. By contrast with the Christian hope of resurrection, it entertains no hope for the continued existence of the body beyond death. Sometimes its hope for an existence beyond death is expressed in terms of reincarnation, usually interpreted as the transmigration of a soul from one body to another – here, clearly, soul and body are viewed as entirely separable, the latter not part of the true essence or existence of the former at all. At other times, an anthropology of the spiritual self specifies its hope for the afterlife rather differently: all hope of continued personal existence is viewed as selfish and arrogant, and the hope which is affirmed is the hope – or rather the conviction – that on death the Spirit which has temporarily manifested itself in a personal form will merge back into the Spirit which is its true substance. As Rosemary Radford Ruether puts it, 'In effect our existence ceases as individuated ego-organism and dissolves back into the cosmic matrix of matter/energy. It is this matrix, rather than our individuated centers of being, that is "everlasting".'[14] What is rightly acknowledged here is that without the body personal identity must cease. Thus by denying the ultimate reality of the body, an anthropology of the spiritual self also denies the ultimate reality of the person. It is thus exposed as an understanding of what it is to be human which willingly embraces the paradox that the goal for human beings is to transcend the human condition altogether. The conclusion is common to most forms of strong dualism.

Spirit in Christian anthropology and Spirit in an anthropology of the spiritual self

As should by now have become clear, Spirit is both what unites and divides a Christian anthropology and an anthropology of the spiritual self. It unites them because they both believe that the human is human only through its relation to Spirit. But it divides them because they conceive of Spirit and its relation to the human in such different ways.

For Christianity, Spirit is the Holy Spirit, God present in and to his creation. Both of the writers I have been considering, Paul and Augustine, are clear that the Holy Spirit is the only possible basis of human life. Both deny the possibility of a human existence independent of God and the Holy Spirit. As Paul asks the Corinthians, 'What have you that you did not receive?' (1 Cor. 4:7). As Augustine exclaims in the *Confessions*, 'I should not exist, unless I existed in you. For all things find in you their origin, their impulse, the centre of their being.'[15] What is left of the human being without the presence of God is, according to both, merely sin: a distortion and corruption of the human person, not the creature as God intended. Only the presence of God to his creatures makes them truly human. The Spirit sustains and transforms both body and soul, beginning his work in this life, and perfecting it in the next.

An anthropology of the spiritual self agrees that the human is only human in relation to the Spirit. It agrees about the reality of the presence of the divine in human life and its constitutive importance to that life. But there the agreement ends. It ends because, as we have seen, an anthropology of the spiritual self does not view the Spirit as perfecting body as well as soul. For Christianity the Spirit is distinct from both mind/soul *and* body/matter. It is related to both as God to his creation. But for an anthropology of the spiritual self the mind/soul is an emanation of Spirit, so

129

Spirit is united with mind/soul and not with body/matter. It does not perfect the body but absorbs it. Whereas in Christianity the Spirit is the animating, perfecting, inspiring and transforming force of the whole creation, material and immaterial, soul and body, in an anthropology of the spiritual self Spirit is related only to mind/consciousness.

A related difference between the two anthropologies is that the Christian one does not view the Spirit as a universal and natural endowment of all things, but as personal gift and communication. As Karl Barth puts it, the Spirit is, 'an absolutely *particular* and specific Spirit, which not only distinguishes itself again and again from all other spirits, but which is seriously to be called "holy".'[16] The Holy Spirit is the gift of God to his creation, God's presence in what he has made. Moreover, it is the Spirit of Jesus Christ. Christ by his resurrection 'became live-giving Spirit' (1 Cor. 15:45). Those who have the Spirit, have the Spirit of Christ. As personal, the Holy Spirit is freely bestowed, it 'blows where it wills'. By contrast, the Spirit of the spiritual self is impersonal and 'natural'. The spiritual self is spiritual not by grace but by nature, and the universe is seen as a natural emanation of Spirit, manifest in a series of fixed and immutable cycles of evolution and dissolution. Its processes do not represent the gracious and free working of a loving God, but invariable and predictable natural processes.

As the free gift of God to the free human person, the Spirit is thus understood by a Christian anthropology as a gift which can be rejected. Those with hearts of stone turn their back on grace, refusing to accept their dependence upon God. Such people wish to rely on their own power, not understanding that all power is from God. As with Adam and Eve, the only possible outcome can be a fall. Consequently, a Christian anthropology admits the reality and danger of human sinfulness in a way which an anthropology of the spiritual self cannot. Because the latter sees the Spirit as a natural endowment of each person, it views each person as naturally and inescapably innocent and good. Unlike Christianity it is incurably (and naively) optimistic. It views the natural and progressive conquest of the person and the universe by Spirit as a inexorable process, and as one which has reached its culmination today in the 'New Age', the Age of the Spirit. For Christianity, however, the Spirit is eschatological: it is the mark and token of the New Age breaking into the old. This present age – and human life – is marked by struggle and warfare between old and new, flesh and spirit, light and darkness. Sin remains a real and terrifying reality of our world which we must face honestly.

The fact that Christianity views the Spirit as gift rather than as a natural endowment of the human person has the further implication that the Spirit is thought to relate God and the believer rather than to absorb the one into the other. Christian theology made this thought precise in thinking through the doctrine of the Trinity and the relation of Father to Son through the Holy Spirit; the persons of the Trinity are understood as unity-in-difference and difference-in-unity. By contrast, an anthropology of the spiritual self views the process in which an individual realises his or her unity with the Spirit as one in which all difference is abolished. Often it is said that realisation occurs when all sense of subject–object differentiation falls away. Likewise, images like that of the river running into the sea or a drop of water into a lake are often used to speak of the individual's 'merging' into the All; on this understanding individuality is abolished, not perfected, in relationship with Spirit.

A further important difference between the two conceptions is that where an anthropology of the spiritual self sees Spirit as the true self of each individual, Christianity understands Spirit not only as the animating and transforming spirit of the individual, but of the group: 'the body of Christ', the 'City of God'. So Jesus promises his disciples, 'where two or three are gathered together in my name, there am I in the midst' (Matt. 18:20). So at Pentecost the Holy Spirit comes upon the 'Church' (which it constitutes), rather than upon a set of individuals. And so the individuals who receive the Spirit do so as parts of a wider whole, limbs of the body of Christ, which is animated as a whole by his Spirit (1 Cor. 12). By contrast, although an anthropology of the spiritual self believes that by realising

131

one's spiritual nature one realises one's unity with all people, this is only a 'spiritual' unity, a matter of consciousness and idea. Christianity finds community not in such an ideal realm, but in the actual groups of men and women who live together in the Spirit: the Church.

On a Christian understanding, then, a person and the wider body of which he or she is a member look 'out' to receive the Spirit as the freely bestowed gift of a loving Creator who will not abandon what he has made. Part of what this means is that the individual Christian may hope to experience the presence of the Spirit directly, possibly by the receipt of charismatic gifts. But just as importantly, it means that the Christian gazes upon the differentiated material and spiritual objects in which the Spirit dwells: upon the Scriptures, upon the sacraments, upon fellow members of the body of Christ, upon the world which God has made. Through such things the Christian hopes to achieve wisdom and attain the Spirit, rather than by going deep within. Expansion is viewed not as an expansion of inner consciousness, but as an expansion of love and sympathy in which things outside the self become 'bound' to the self.[17] By contrast, an anthropology of the spiritual self directs the salvific gaze within. It believes that truth and goodness are to be found in the plenitude of one's inner self. It thereby commends an inwardness which Christianity condemns: Luther speaks of being *incurvatum in se*, curved in upon oneself, as the state of sin; by contrast an anthropology of the spiritual self sees it as the beginning of wisdom.

Different anthropologies, different conceptions of the good life

The differences between an anthropology of the spiritual self and a Christian anthropology have important practical implications. These different understandings of the person give rise to significantly different pictures of what constitutes a good human life, and it is here perhaps that what is at stake in the debate between the two shows itself most clearly.

132

The most striking idea about the good life which arises from an anthropology of the spiritual self is the idea that there is a separate dimension of human life which may be referred to as the 'spiritual life'. This is thought of as a sphere with its own practices and techniques, the cultivation of which is central to the good life. The implicit dualism of the anthropology of the spiritual self clearly lies behind these ideas: once imagine that one has a true spiritual self which is different from one's everyday material, mundane and impermanent self, and it is but a short step to imagine that one has a spiritual life richer and more real than one's everyday, mundane and workaday life within the material world. It is then natural to imagine that this spiritual life can be cultivated with the aid of different knowledges and sets of practices.

A plethora of different spiritual technologies have emerged to guide the spiritual self, some distinctive to different teachers or esoteric groups, some more widely accessible through the burgeoning corpus of spiritual literature available today. But for all their variety, these spiritual technologies all seem to share certain central features, features closely linked to an anthropology of the spiritual self. Because the latter is regarded as first and foremost an inner and private self – mind, consciousness or Spirit rather than matter – the spiritual life is correspondingly viewed primarily as an individual and private matter, having to do primarily with consciousness and mental states. This explains why meditation in its various forms has become such a key spiritual practice for the spiritual self. Various forms of ritualistic practice such as deep trance, 'trance dance', and poetic chant are also growing in popularity. But all share the same aim as meditation, an aim often expressed as 'expansion of consciousness'. As one recent advocate of feminist spirituality puts it, 'witches practice a craft, the aim of which is to put people on better terms with *their own mental life.*'[18]

As I have mentioned, much recent Christianity has been greatly affected by such ideas and practices. It has embraced the idea that cultivation of one's inner, spiritual life lies at the heart of the good life, and it has produced its

133

own spiritual literature. And all the denominations, Catholic as well as Protestant, display an increasing concern with the individual and his or her private spiritual development. The recent popularity of schemes of personality typing within Christianity are one witness to this concern; another is the growing popularity of spiritual retreats where the individual can receive direction for his or her individual spiritual life.[19] Some forms of Christianity have even adopted forms of meditation. Yet these developments have really only taken off since the last war. For 19 centuries, Christianity produced few equivalent 'spiritual techniques', and no exact parallels. Why? Because Christianity viewed the good life as the life of transformation of the whole human being, their community, and the world. The good life concerned the whole person, not just a separate spiritual dimension of the person, and it concerned the whole world, material and immaterial. The entire differentiated reality of God's creation was seen as in travail as it awaited redemption; and the good life was the life of participation in this transformation.

Rather than commending mental exercises and practices, then, Christianity has typically fostered very different 'spiritual practices', prayer and worship in particular. They differ from meditative practices in the first place because they involve a turning without rather than a turning within; an opening of heart, mind and life to God. And they differ in the second place because of their communal rather than individual nature. So the primary context of both prayer and worship in the Christian tradition is that of the community of believers, the Church. Individual prayer and worship are of course also part of Christian practice, but they are to be understood as secondary, as 'take-aways' from the Church.[20] Even the lone Christian prays in awareness that his or her prayers are joined with the prayers of the universal Church, a Church which spreads across time as well as space.

In addition, rather than concentrating upon the cultivation of one's spiritual self and the spiritual sphere, Christian worship has generally been thought of as inseparably bound up with ethical action. The Christian sees the good life as a life in which love of self, God and neighbour are inseparably bound up with one another.[21] The good life cannot therefore be confined to a private spiritual sphere, but will necessarily involve the public world, the world which God has made, a world worthy of love and care in all its parts and in all its concrete particularity. Moreover, the Christian has guidance in the living of the ethical life in a way the spiritual self does not. The gaze of the worshipper is a gaze without, a gaze directed upon God, made known through his deeds in the world, the commandments he has given, through his Word made flesh, and through his saints. So the gaze provides standards by which the good life can be measured and inspired. By contrast, the gaze within of the spiritual self has no guide except the self itself. As a result, its emphasis is upon the freedom of the individual to find their own truth 'within' and to express it.[22] Integrity (self-consistency) becomes the chief virtue. Of course, Christianity also has an anti-ethical and libertarian tradition centred on belief in the guidance of the Holy Spirit in the life of each believer, but it always has a 'check'. This check is Christ: since the Holy Spirit is the Spirit of Christ, that which is not in conformity with Jesus Christ's earthly life, death and resurrection cannot be the good.

Finally, it should be mentioned that a Christian anthropology and an anthropology of the spiritual self give rise to two very different ideals of the good life because of their different attitudes to the body. Since the latter believes that the ideal for a human is to merge into Spirit, it is forced to conclude that the ideal of human life is to become other-than-human: to become divine. By contrast, because a Christian anthropology sees the body (albeit the transformed body) as part of redeemed human existence, it does not hope or expect the limitations which are such a defining part of what it is to be human to be dissolved. The body limits a person within time and space, it limits a person to a particular identity, and it distinguishes the human from God as well as from other sorts of creature. All this Christianity accepts: limitation is viewed not as hindrance but as part of the perfection of the creature made and redeemed by God. So the Christian ideal is not to escape from the human condition nor to become a God, but to become truly human, to become truly what God intended.

Conclusion: 'very God and very Man'

I have spoken at some length about how the two anthropologies I have been considering are divided by their different understandings of the Spirit; but I have also hinted that their common emphasis upon the importance of the Spirit in human life is an important point of agreement between them. Indeed, it may even be that by revivifying this emphasis an anthropology of the spiritual self has done a great service to Christianity in reminding it of neglected aspects of its own tradition. As Karl Barth suggested in relation to Schleiermacher (whom he suspected of formulating an early version of what I have called the spiritual self), he and his latter-day followers had done Christians the service of reminding them of the importance of their neglected 'third article': belief in the Holy Spirit.[23] And yet, as I have been at pains to show in this chapter, the ways in which an anthropology of the spiritual self and a Christian anthropology work out their doctrines of the Spirit and of the closeness between human and divine seem not just different, but ultimately irreconcilable.

Nowhere can this basic disagreement between the two anthropologies be seen more clearly than in relation to an orthodox (Chalcedonian) understanding of Jesus Christ. For it is here that Christianity's anti-dualism in the sense both of its holistic understanding of the human, and its refusal to set the human and divine wholly at odds with one another, comes into sharpest focus, and so here that the two anthropologies stand in sharpest contrast. The orthodox understanding of Jesus as 'very Man and very God', truly divine and truly human, makes vivid the revolutionary idea that the reality of God the Logos may not be such as to wipe out the reality of the human, but to constitute it. The natures of God and the human are understood not as mutually exclusive, not as competing, but as able to exist together 'without confusion, without transmutation, without division'.[24] Despite the eclecticism and tolerance of the New Spirituality and its anthropology of the spiritual self, this Chalcedonian Christology remains its sticking point. It shuns the affirmation that the man Jesus Christ can be God, for it cannot accept such a 'localisation' of God, it cannot accept the idea of a fleshly and 'personed' God. It can accept that the Spirit underlies all things and makes all divine, but it cannot accept that the Spirit can be present at particular times and places, transforming differentiated reality and uniting with material and bodily realities. It cannot accept that God and the human can exist in the most intimate union without the latter being absorbed into the former.

So for this, as well as for the many other reasons outlined above, I believe that ultimately an anthropology of the spiritual self and a Christian anthropology must part company. I have tried to show that the former is deficient both in its ontology and its ethic. In encouraging the impossible and misconceived aim of leaving behind the concrete particulars of the world and one's embodied individuality in order to merge with some deeper, spiritual reality, it gives rise to some of the more troubling pathologies of human life today, pathologies I have tried to hint at above. It gives rise to the dangerous sense that there may be some reality greater and more valuable than the human: and in a century which has witnessed unparalleled acts of genocide, any such sense must surely be treated with the very highest suspicion. It gives rise to a dualism which seems increasingly pervasive, and which encourages the view that my only true reality is my private, spiritual reality, and that what I do with my body is of small consequence. Such dualism too easily exalts the 'inner self' and leaves the public and everyday world and our action within it outside the realm of the truly significant. Finally, it gives rise to a libertarian ethic which seeks all values 'within', and places the highest value upon 'integrity', 'being true to oneself', 'expressing oneself', and 'doing it my way', but which underestimates the reality of sin and too easily leaves people not free but trapped in a world of moral confusion.

I have tried to show that Christians possess a powerful

137

tradition of thought about the human person which immunises against all these pathologies by its refusal to spiritualise human reality and by its insistence that the goal of human life is the goal of becoming fully human. This anthropology understands Spirit as the Holy Spirit, the presence of a personal God to his creation, a presence in which that creation dwells and a presence which makes possible its concrete and differentiated God-given reality: soul and body, mind and matter, flesh and spirit. On this understanding all life exists in the Spirit and is what it is through the Spirit. Through the Spirit the creation becomes as God intended. Human beings become truly human. Not other than they are, but as God intended them to be. They become human as the human has been revealed in Jesus Christ: completely and utterly of God, and at the same time completely and utterly human. Completely for God, completely for others and, in this, completely for themselves. I have tried to show that the Christian Gospel is a Gospel of a God who is for humanity without reserve and whose presence in the Spirit does not destroy human beings, but makes them fully human: in all their concrete and embodied particularity.

And through all this I have tried to play out in some small way the theme of this volume, which I glossed in my opening remarks: that serious, open, loving and critical attentiveness to our tradition can free us from an angry reaction against what has immediately preceded, and give us a critical purchase on the currently fashionable.

Notes to Chapter 6

1 It is possible to see this by consulting almost any piece of literature associated with the movement. A useful anthology of New Age texts is that edited by William Bloom, *The New Age: an anthology of essential reading* (London, Rider, 1991).

2 As the feminist theologian Rosemary Radford Ruether puts it, 'If a [religious] symbol does not speak authentically to experience, it becomes dead or must be altered to provide a new meaning', *Sexism and God-Talk: towards a feminist theology* (London, SCM, 1983), p. 13.

3 Paul Heelas' recent book, *The New Age Movement: the celebration of the self and the sacralisation of modernity* (Oxford, Blackwell, 1996), argues

this case in close relation to the teachings and pratices of the movement. As the subtitle of that book suggests, Heelas regards the New Age as part and parcel of that central strand of the modern project which he calls the 'turn to the self'. He argues that the New Age is the most significant religious manifestation of this turn and in this sense is a 'sacralisation of modernity'.

4 Mary Grey, *The Wisdom of Fools? Seeking Revelation for Today* (London, SPCK, 1993), p. 62. Author's italics.

5 On this last development see, for example. Paul Heelas, "God's Company": New Age ethics and the Bank of Credit and Commerce International', in *Religion Today* 8, (1), Autumn/Winter 1992, pp. 1–4

6 I have argued this at greater length in my article, 'Spiritualising the Sacred: a critique of feminist theology', forthcoming in *Modern Theology,* 1997.

7 See, e.g., Fox's *Original Blessing* (Santa Fe, Vere and Co., 1983).

8 So, e.g., he says of death, the sundering of soul from body, that 'this violent sundering of two elements, which are conjoined and interwoven in a human being, is bound to be a harsh and unnatural experience' (*City of God*, Book XIII, Ch. 6).

9 See Paul Ramsey's 'Human Sexuality in the History of Redemption' in *Journal of Religious Ethics*, 16, 1 (Spring 1988), pp. 56–86. Here Ramsey argues that Augustine, though he did not escape all error in his discussion of sex and the body, at least viewed both within the context of the history of redemption: something which contemporary treatments rarely do.

10 Augustine's guiding principle in answering these questions is that the resurrection body will be transformed into the perfected version of the earthly body: transformed, but not out of recognition. So he reassures his audience, for example, that 'fat and thin people have no need to fear that at the resurrection they will be the kind of people they would not have chosen to be in this life, if they had had the chance' (*City of God*, Book XXII, Ch. 19).

11 Thus in the evolutionary schemes which are typical of spiritual monism in its many forms, matter is often said to be an involution of Spirit. It is not something which is good or real in itself, but only by virtue of its being a manifestation of Spirit, and its ultimate destiny is to dissolve back into the Spirit from which it derived.

12 This slogan appears at the end of the nineteenth century, the time when clear statements of an anthropology of the spiritual self first begin to emerge at the centre of alternative religious systems. These systems – the most notable early example of which is Theosophy – nearly all have roots in Spiritualism, the movement which swept the USA and Europe in the second half of the nineteenth century, and which believed that the human mind, because of its connection with the spiritual world, was able to influence phenomena within this world. See, for example, Janet Oppenheim, *The Other World: Spiritualism and psychical research in England 1850–1911* (Cambridge, Cambridge University Press, 1985).

13 Mary Baker Eddy's Christian Science movement was one of the earliest and most influential of such systems of spiritual healing. Typically, Eddy (like Madame Blavatsky, the founder of Theosophy) was influenced by Spiritualism, and in particular by the spiritualist healing theories of P. Quimby. Her *Science and Health* was first published in 1875.

14 *Sexism and God-Talk*, op. cit., p. 257.

15 *Confessions*, Book I, 2. Augustine here quotes Rom. 11:36 and Jer. 23:24.

16 'Concluding Unscientific Postscript on Schleiermacher', reprinted in the reader edited by Clifford Green, *Karl Barth: the theologian of freedom* (Minneapolis, Fortress Press, 1991), p. 86.

17 The hymn 'St Patrick's Breastplate' speaks of this binding in memorable terms: the Christian binds to him or herself not just 'the strong name of the Trinity', but Christ's life and death, the power of the angels, the sun and stars, the stable earth and deep salt sea, and 'Confessors' faith, Apostle's word,/ the Patriarchs' prayers, the prophets' scrolls./ All good deeds done unto the Lord/ And purity of virgin souls'.

18 Naomi Goldenberg, *Changing of the Gods: feminism and the end of traditional religions* (Beacon Press, Boston, 1979), p. 91. Italics mine.

19 Some retreats now centre around personality tests, and there is a large amount of literature interpreting personality tests for Christians, relating their outcomes to prayer life etc. The Myers Briggs and Enneagram personality sorters are the most commonly employed. A representative example of the literature is Bruce Duncan's *Praying Your Way: your personality and God* (London, Darton, Longman and Todd, 1993).

20 This image is used by the liturgust George Guiver in his *Everyday God* (London, SPCK, 1994).

21 This belief is most clearly and importantly enshrined in the 'double commandment' to love God and neighbour as one's self (Matt. 22:36–40 and parallels).

22 Such an ethic has been described by Charles Taylor as 'an ethic of authenticity' and a 'expressivist ethic'. See Taylor, *Sources of the Self: the making of modern identity* (Cambridge, Cambridge University Press, 1989); and Taylor, *The Ethics of Authenticity* (London, Harvard University Press, 1991).

23 See 'Concluding Unscientific Postscript on Schleiermacher', op. cit., esp. pp. 88–90.

24 From the Definition of Chalcedon (451).

7 Personal and Cosmic: The Two Moods

Angela Tilby

Christian self-understanding is inevitably affected by contemporary understandings of the natural world. This has been true since the beginning of the Christian era. The early apologists, for example, incorporated Stoic and Platonic views of nature into their thinking with varying degrees of critical insight. The problem has always been where to draw the line, to discover how far Christian belief can be expressed through such understandings, and when it becomes irretrievably subverted by them. Our present view of the natural world is dominated by Darwin's evolutionary biology. Since the time of Darwin, the majority of Christian theologians have shown a marked reluctance to think constructively about the doctrine of creation. Creation has been left to the scientists, while the theologians marked out the self and society for their territory. Ethics, spirituality, ecclesiology and social issues have occupied the agenda. There has been a retreat from the attempt to articulate a religious cosmology embracing creation, sin and redemption. Even those who have tried to make sense of Darwin – the process theologians, for example – have assumed that theology could only be the handmaid of supposedly superior scientific interpretations of the universe. Yet, time and again, these supposedly scientific interpretations overreach themselves, driving theology into blind alleys.

I will illustrate this by examining two scientific interpretations of the natural world which have provoked a theological response. These interpretations are reflected in

141

different moods towards nature. I say moods, because it is not the general facts of evolution which are in question but the interpretation of those facts, and the mood and feeling tone within which different interpretations are expressed.

The first mood suggests that the human condition is one of tragic alienation. We are disconnected from nature by the very consciousness which enables us to reflect on it. The second mood suggests that we are embedded *in* nature, and that consciousness, including spiritual awareness, is a natural part of the web of connections which binds us to the universe. The boundaries between selves are fuzzy and permeable.

I want to explore the thinking behind these moods in some detail and then consider what happens when theologians mistakenly use them as their starting point for understanding creation. So, a brief outline of arguments put forward by two creative and literary men of science, Jacques Monod and Gregory Bateson. Monod speaks as a molecular biologist, Bateson as an ethnologist and psychiatrist. The two wrote within a few years of each other, both within a Darwinian framework. Yet their reading of the natural world, and the spiritual and moral applications of living in such a world, are quite different.

First, Monod. His famous essay, Chance and Necessity[1], came from lectures delivered in California in 1969. These comprise an elegant exposition of the nature of living organisms. Monod argued that the implication of Darwin's theory of evolution, once its mechanisms had been grasped, was that the strangeness and variety of life was no more than the product of blind chance and brute necessity. Once this principle had been absorbed it could be seen that there was no room for what Monod called animism. He chose the word deliberately, to provoke, by pointing to what he regarded as the primitive nature of religious belief. There can be neither 'soul' nor explanation in a world constructed by chance and necessity. Monod goes on to argue that it is the role of science to attack all value systems which are based on animism. The 'old covenant' between man and nature has broken down. Knowledge and values can no longer be seen as coming from the same source. He warns us that the educative role of science is not complete if it leaves people enjoying the fruits of science without hearing its deeper, atheistic message. Science exists to strip us of illusion, to bring us to the recognition that we are alone in a blind and meaningless universe. For many of our contemporaries Monod's reductionist atheism is still scientific orthodoxy. It is greeted now, as it was then, with a kind of grim delight. One of the most interesting contemporary exponents of Monod's approach, Richard Dawkins, is a popular and well-regarded radio and television panellist, pundit and newspaper columnist.

Gregory Bateson's *Steps to an Ecology of Mind*[2] was written in 1971. It was followed by a more popular version, *Mind and Nature*[3], in 1979. Both books were essays about ideas, biology, the structure of the mind and cybernetics. Bateson's interests are primarily *ecological*. How do ideas interact with one another? Is there a mental equivalent to natural selection which allows for the survival of some ideas and the death of others? How does the universe produce minds? And how is the universe patterned in the structures of the mind? Such questions reveal that Bateson is looking less for causes than for relationships and symmetries. Where Monod is reductionist, Bateson is holistic. An example of the Bateson approach is in his description of an informal course he used to teach for psychiatric residents. It once included what he describes as a 'catechism' of significant questions. These ranged from 'What is a *sacrament*?' to 'What is *entropy*?' and 'What is *play*?' Bateson's interests include anthropology, linguistics, philosophy and religion, but his grounding, like Monod's, is in evolutionary biology.

Both Monod and Bateson accept an evolutionary account of nature. Both believe that the kind of knowledge science can give is an essential component of what it means to be human. Both allow science a degree of moral mission. Both celebrate the human capacity to play with ideas, or just to play, to reflect and to live as a subject.

But what is more noticeable about the two writers is their irreconcilably different attitudes to the natural world. This is revealed in the style of their writing as much as in its

143

content. Monod's style is spare, his structure both logical and lucid. He expounds the science, he turns to rhetoric to deliver his atheistic gospel. As he sees it, man is the victim of real stress and distress. This is because he finds that he belongs simultaneously to the animal kingdom and to the kingdom of ideas, and it is this dual membership which both tears him apart and enriches him. Both art and love emerge from the irretrievable loss of a sense of wholeness. He is no longer one with nature. There is no world soul, no spirits in the forest. Monod writes with a passion which is almost mystical in its negativity. He ends with the stark challenge of our aloneness:

> The ancient covenant is in pieces; man at last knows that he is alone in the unthinking immensity of the universe, out of which he emerged only by chance. Neither his destiny, nor his duty have been written down. The kingdom above, or the darkness below: it is for him to choose.

Bateson, on the other hand, does not see our position in the universe as tragic. His style is relaxed. He is both personal and anecdotal. He tells stories about stories and describes computers that tell stories. Mind, for him, has a place in the universe; it is part of the universe's pattern, and belongs here as much as stars and snowflakes and crabs' claws. He reads nature not as a sermon but as a song. He likes jokes, diagrams and puns. Above all he stresses that animals like us are embedded in the natural world, so we are not strangers. Nor are we alone because we are mirrored in the universe *as persons*. It is not only the mechanisms of our nature which we see in the stars and the atoms. It is the very things which make us *us*:

> It was not the crudest, the simplest, the most animalistic and primitive aspects of the human species that were reflected in the natural phenomena. It was rather, the more complex, the aesthetic, the intricate, and the elegant aspects of people that reflected nature ... roots of human symmetry, beauty and ugliness, aesthetics, the human being's very aliveness and little bit of wisdom.

This being so, it is not a strange or fanciful conceit to look for a theory which embraces culture as well as genetics, thinking as well as natural selection. If genetic replication (necessity) and mutation (chance) are the driving tools of biological evolution, then intellectual rigour and imagination are the tools of mental endeavour. In place of Monod's bracing atheism Bateson seeks to recall us to a sense of the sacred unity of all being:

> Most of us have lost that sense of unity of biosphere and humanity which would bind and reassure us with an affirmation of beauty . . . we have lost the core of Christianity. We have lost Shiva, the dancer of Hinduism, whose dance at the trivial level is both creation and destruction, but in whole is beauty.

To draw out the essential contrast between the two: Bateson is aware that Darwin attempted to exclude mind from the universe. For him, this is a basic error. Monod, on the other hand, is rigorous in following Darwin at this point. The human condition is desperately lonely because in the last analysis mind *is* anomalous. It is not necessary. It does not belong. It is a product of chance, brute and blind.

For Bateson, chance is not quite blind. Evolution itself is what he calls a *stochastic* process. Random, chance events are the raw material of a selective process which allows only certain outcomes to endure. Those outcomes are ones which will last. They have a quality of beauty and integrity and fittingness which secures their survival above their rivals. To say that 'what lasts is what lasts' is, of course, a tautology, and Bateson is aware of this. Nature, he insists, is just that, 'a self-healing tautology'. Thought resembles evolution in employing both random elements and a selective process that prefers some outcomes to others. The universe is patterned, destined for relationship. Where Monod hopes to teach us to abandon all our animisms, Bateson encourages us to return to a view of the universe as ensouled. Nature is ripe for re-enchantment.

For Monod we are still capable of a kind of transcendence in spite of the loneliness of our condition. Simply because we are the only thinking beings we have heroic possibilities. Individuals and communities can choose their actions. They are responsible moral agents. Where then, do

145

values come from, and how are they legitimated? Monod argues that true knowledge is ignorant of values, but this does not mean that human beings can live without them. He suggests that it is a human choice to elect knowledge itself as a supreme value. This choice brings us to the only transcendence we can know. We can choose to build a humane society based on an ethic of knowledge. For him this will be a form of ethical socialism, which he commends as both rational and idealistic. This ideal must go beyond the desires of the individual to the point even of self-sacrifice if this is necessary.

Bateson is less interested in politics and ethics and more interested in the general concept of wisdom. He believes that the loss of wisdom is evident in our systems of education. The reductive, analytical approach, if it is all that there is on offer, leads to boredom and intellectual sterility. He is a kind of neo-neo Platonist. What is more important than a reductionist analysis of the things we find in nature is a grasp of the *pattern that connects*. It is characteristic of Bateson to pose questions like: 'What pattern connects the crab to the lobster and the orchid to the primrose and all four of them to me?' The search for a pattern does not involve an analysis in terms of quantity, but a capacity for empathy and recognition. Bateson wants to turn the conventional logic of scientific reductionism on its head. He believes that it contains a fundamental mistake in excluding mind as an explanation of nature. The consequences of this mistake are all around us in 'greed, monstrous overgrowth, war, tyranny, and pollution. In this sense our premises are daily demonstrated as false.' As a result we have lost the sense of aesthetic unity which allows nature and thought to be inextricably linked.

The hierarchical structure of human thought as it moves from random reactions to more comprehensive understanding is an expression of the hierarchies inherent in nature. There *is* a great chain of being. The process of evolution is not linear, but spiral. Not from the crudely simple to the complex, but an interlocking network of complexity and simplicity. Bateson's agenda is to elucidate the 'sacred unity of the biosphere'. He draws on religious insights but

146

believes that he gives them a more solid foundation in science than has previously been possible. To live wisely within nature is to live within limits. We have no choice about this; it is an illusion to regard ourselves as anomalous beings, free to choose our destiny. This is the mistake of the old reductionist science. Nature is always bigger than us and we are only a part:

> Evolution was the history of how organisms learned more tricks for controlling the environment; and man had better tricks than any other creature. But that arrogant scientific philosophy is now obsolete, and in its place there is a discovery that man is only part of larger systems and that the part can never control the whole.

If this is true, then what appears to be individual choice and freedom may turn out to be adaptive behaviour, required by our environment. None of us is as free as he or she thinks. 'We are not by any means the captains of our souls.' Our genes create us, our relationships confine us in various ways. Nature has its own logic, its own tendencies towards certain outcomes, many of which may be unknowable by us. But we do mirror nature in as much as we are beings who learn. Evolution and learning are parts of the same single, natural process. At one point Bateson ponders whether it is of any importance that the right things are done for the right reasons. Nature will get there anyway, wherever there is. The tautology of lasting outcomes that last will heal itself. The tears in the fabric of nature caused by random processes cleanse and renew nature. In such a system death has a positive role: however good the man, he becomes a toxic nuisance if he stays around too long . . .' The process by which nature heals itself may well include the extinction of the human species. Bateson does not seem particularly troubled by this eventuality. Bateson's vision of the world is sympathetic to the religious instinct. It is sensitive to beauty and order and to emotions such as awe and wonder. His mysticism leads him towards pantheism rather than theism or atheism. It is nature itself which transcends human beings, nature itself which teaches us humility, nature which judges, cleanses and may finally destroy us, but if and when it does so, the rent we have left in its fabric will be healed and the process of life and thought will continue in new ways.

What effects have these related but opposing pictures of humanity and nature had on our theology and spirituality? I believe they have been devastating. Not so much because of the hostility which both pictures carry for orthodox Christianity, but more for the way in which Christian thinkers, starting from such interpretations as givens, have incorporated them, uncritically, into the Christian world-view. Both approaches have driven Christians to present their beliefs principally in this-wordly terms. The reasons for this are obvious: the intellectual climate is hostile to the notion that the reasons for the world's existence lie outside itself. Once it is accepted as an apologetic *strategy* to play down the transcendence of God and the hope of heaven, it soon becomes difficult to remember how central such beliefs are. Much contemporary Christianity lacks any vivid expectation of personal life after death. Salvation or even resurrection are often treated as metaphors indicating hope in a particular kind of social future, or a transformed personal attitude. Christian thinkers have fallen into the trap of believing that they must demonstrate as much, or more, scepticism about the difficult bits of belief as their most negative critics.

The atheistic world-view of Monod had and continues to have a huge influence. Our education systems, not only in the sciences, but also in many arts subjects, are based on the premise that the only wisdom available is the sum of our knowledge and technical skill. It has often been observed that it is when the full blast of the reductionist world-view hits children – usually at between ten and twelve – that quite sophisticated religious belief often gives way to scepticism. Attacks like Monod's on 'animism' put Christianity on the defensive. The tendency among Christians is to try to incorporate the atheistic critique into Christian thinking rather than to confront it head on.

In the 1960s the Church made various attempts to pare down, to simplify and to explain its beliefs and practices. It was considered important to condemn superstition and naïvety in believing. Some forms of biblical criticism were reductionism brought into theology, an attempt to identify the earliest units of tradition and build a new 'purer', more believable theology out of the non-miraculous remainder. The stress on the importance of ethics, although it can hardly be shown to arise naturally from science like Monod's, also put pressure on the Church to demonstrate that its Gospel was benign and humane. This was not a time when it was easy for the Church to say deeply unpopular things, to speak *contra mundum*, against the world, or about *another* world.

Thanks to thinkers like Monod, it is now taken for granted that the test of true religion is that it benefits humankind. The Church's agenda had to prove itself worthy of modernity in the high court of ethical humanism and socialism. Heroic individuals were acceptable. Monod himself commended self-sacrifice as the ultimate ethical action. This has echoes in a kind of heroic Christology which had a huge influence on a whole generation. Jesus Christ was 'the man for others', the selfless individual who sacrificed himself for the world. His was an *example* to be followed and emulated. There were several important attempts to restate Christianity in terms that would meet the critique of thinkers like Monod.

The most revealing example was Harvey Cox's *The Secular City*,[4] which was written several years before *Chance and Necessity*. Cox anticipated Monod in prophesying the end of all animisms. Unlike Monod, though, he argued that the disenchantment of nature was not a rejection but a necessary outcome of a biblical world-view. The death of the sacred was actively encouraged by the Creator God of Genesis. In the biblical creation account he discerns a radical de-mythologising of the natural world. Cox wrote before Monod, but he knew the agenda which Monod would present. In response he drew on iconoclastic tendencies within the biblical tradition to encourage believing man to feel at home in his new alien environment. A studied coolness was the best possible defence against the erosion of faith – a coolness which incorporated the arguments of atheism, while not apparently bowing to its conclusions. What is startling is the disengagement with which Cox writes. Where Monod seems to appreciate the tragedy of the loss of the sacred, Cox is simply unfazed. He is playboy become theologian.

The Secular City is a celebration of what was, in the late 1960s, modernity. It was right to predict the increasing urbanisation of our culture, but Cox did not anticipate the subsequent attempts to re-sacralise nature as the ecological and feminist movements got under way. Cox can still put human beings in the centre of the stage. Like Monod, Cox would have called himself a humanist, but unlike Monod, he believed that our mandate to be human came from God. There was not much point, though, in the rest of creation. It was there to serve human needs, but Cox did not debate the question of whether it had any purpose in itself. He noticed that in the Secular City nouns became verbs. It was natural to think in functional, rather than ontological or metaphysical terms. He also suggested that city life brought about an end to tribal relationships. Tribal man, he suggested, was hardly a 'self' at all. He does not live *in* a tribe, he lives as an *expression* of the tribe. Man and nature, the animals and gods are bound together in a continuous life process. Sacred meaning runs through the whole, just below the surface. What begins to end this sacred unity, according to Cox, is currency and language. The city continues the process of 'separating nature from God and distinguishing man from nature'. Nature is not a divine entity and man is nor a mere expression of nature. He is instead called to free decision and free response. The cost of freedom is the breakdown of given intimate connections between people, and this, too, he welcomed. Our intimate relationships could now be relationships of choice rather than necessity. Most of our relationships would not be of an 'I-thou' nature but of an 'I-you' nature. 'I-you' relationships were free associations of equals, interdependent but not intimate. The culture of the organisation replaced the culture of the tribe. Provocatively, he suggested that 'organisation man' had evolved from the Gospel call to free decision. Cox's strongest term of contempt is 'immature'. Part of mature man's relationship with God should be as co-worker. Man was the measure of all things in the Secular City: 'We experience the universe as the city of man. It is a field of human exploration and endeavour from which the gods have fled.'

What is difficult in Cox's account is to assign any real meaning to the word 'God'. There is no obvious space in the Secular City for sacraments or prayer or contemplation. The functionalism and pragmatism of the city arise from the fact that we find the world sufficient and reliable. To 'need' God, is, presumably, an expression of immaturity, since all decisions of importance are handed back to us. Where, then, is God in the Secular City? Cox argues for a transcendent God, and yet the quiet slippage from high transcendence to overt atheism is almost inevitable. Cox recognises the difficulty and suggests rather lamely that everyone must decide for himself whether the God of the Bible is really *there*, or is just a rich and fruitful way of talking about ourselves. This also is a free choice and is part of what it means to be human. The only place where we might speak meaningfully of God is where we find ourselves up against it, in the helplessness of extreme experience and as we contemplate death. Cox has very little to say about death, whereas Monod's essay seems to be haunted by it. Both have probably ceased to believe in any kind of afterlife, but Monod at least still knows what he is missing.

Creation is linked in Cox's thought to human freedom and secularity. The world is simply what it is and does not contain hidden or coded sacral meanings which would compel our belief or evoke our awe. The emphasis is on God's transcendence and hiddenness. The world that we find ourselves in is the sphere of human choice, and we build here a kingdom or a chaos. Almost prophetically Cox anticipates Monod: 'Neither his destiny, nor his duty have been written down. The kingdom above, or the darkness below: it is for him to choose.'

The choice of destiny was serious not only for the individual but for humanity. Cox was, after all, writing when the world was still gripped by the shadow of the nuclear bomb. Redemption, in such a world, is expressed as liberation from the fear of threat or disaster. It was important to

151

believe that peace was possible and could be achieved. As individuals what we needed to be set free from are the limitations of religion, class and ethnicity, from injustice in the workplace and in the global community. This is clearly this-worldly salvation. The role of the Church is of a small-scale voluntary organisation acting as an enabling servant to look after human needs as and when they arise. The Church's model human being is, not surprisingly, Jesus of Nazareth, who is depicted, characteristically, as a genuinely 'free' man. Both individuals and communities are seen as responsible moral agents. The sphere of our moral life is public and political. The liberating Gospel requires fearless engagement in the political process in which our primary concern should not be to preserve either our consciences or our innocence.

The full drama of Cox's arguments did not ring true in a British context. It was not until the 1980s that we produced anything like the 'enterprise culture' that Cox knew in American cities, by which time the religious agenda itself had moved on. In Britain the churches of the Cox/Monod era had been involved in the post-war restructuring of society, where they had carried considerable influence in education policy and the media. The 1960s were a new era of scandals, affluence and youth culture. It was a decade which consciously separated itself from tradition, where confidence in the new sprang from a violent loss of confidence in the old. There was certainly a sense that a new society was emerging. This was the decade of Coventry Cathedral, of the demolition of Victorian city centres, of comprehensive schools and of a massive social housing programme. It was the era of the famous Harold Wilson speech about the future being forged in the 'white heat of technology'. The churches too began to envision a new future for themselves. The given parochial structures could not be the only ones for the new era. There was an outburst of interest in sector ministry, in industrial chaplaincy, in 'worker-priests'. There was confidence that the engagement of the Church with the secular world would be seen as 'relevant' and might even stir the uncommitted to take an interest in religion. But the pressures of the reductionist critique of religion, with its stress on ethical engagement and self-sacrifice, took their toll. It may have been difficult to articulate a sense of sin, but that did not stop a sense of guilt. The image of Jesus, 'the man for others' – selfless, free, perfectly integrated and endlessly self-giving – was an impossible ideal for the average clergyman, social worker, teacher or missionary. The heroic ideal was unattainable. Worse, to many the whole secular Christian package was deeply unattractive. The moral intensity exacerbated anxiety; the loss of old words and hopes, the sweeping away of the language of reasonable certainty left people on their own, struggling to be good in the absence of grace. Christianity began to be perceived as thin, shallow and uninteresting, a gloss, and no more, on moral commitment.

In London, Manchester, Glasgow and Liverpool ancient slums were cleared away and replaced with proud new tower blocks. The chapel of King's College, Cambridge was very nearly converted into a public swimming pool. Barbara Castle declared the new town Kirkby in Merseyside to be 'the new Jerusalem'. Ten years later it had become a hell of privation and growing unemployment. Twenty years later the tower blocks were blown up. Technopolis had turned out to be not the city of God, but a true wilderness. The desacralisation of nature had led to the desecration of the spirit.

The shift between views of nature did not happen neatly in time. There are plenty of popular scientists who continue Monod's atheistic and moral mission. But the more holistic picture has established itself, if not in the bastions of orthodoxy, then at least in the popular mind. What has caused this change is the widespread belief, based on some plausible evidence, that humanity is destroying its own environment.

The agenda set out by thinkers like Bateson has been echoed by many in the Christian world and in the half-Christian penumbra. It speaks to those disturbed by our ecological problems, to feminists, to those concerned to articulate a 'creation theology'. His interests resonate with new initiatives in contemplation and liturgy, in dialogue between faiths, in the 'cosmic' Christ, in the doctrine of the

153

Trinity as offering a more 'related' model of God than is usual within monotheism. He has something to say to the critique of individualism in contemporary Christianity, to the therapies which seek to 'heal' the mind/body split, to the formation of 'alternative' communities. It is hard to pick out a single individual who has become a Christian spokesperson for the holistic approach, but Matthew Fox probably comes closest. Fox draws on the thought of Thomas Berry, who is indebted to Teilhard de Chardin. Fox believes that what is wrong with contemporary Christianity is the doctrine of original sin. This has distorted the Christian message, putting too much emphasis on what is wrong with us, and not enough on the mystery and dignity of our creation. He has heard the guilt-provoking call to heroism that comes from the earlier scientific picture and can see the distortions it has led to. Fox aims to construct a more playful, emotionally liberated sense of what it is to be a Christian.

In doing so he has to face the question of what we say about creation and redemption when we know we are *embedded in* nature? In answer he draws on the various process theologies which suggest that God accompanies us in the process of becoming. Process theologies are pantheistic, or at least pan-entheistic, though the difference is not all that clear. From this emerges an ethic of caring and preservation. The world is precious because it is God's work of art. Damaging nature is harming what God is making of himself. It is a short step from this conviction to the assumption that the destruction of the rain-forest is a kind of global crucifixion.

It is worth reminding ourselves that it really is an innovatory move to identify God with nature in this way. For an earlier age 'nature' was what was given. It could be friend or foe, but whichever it was it was not divine. Christian views of nature are inherited from the Wisdom tradition and from Genesis. St Paul follows these in stressing nature's dependence on God. Nature has no ultimate meaning within itself, though as a sign of God's creativity and goodness it could be thought of as having its own voice to praise God. In this limited sense, nature is animated, en-souled.

But nature is as mortal as we are, 'subject to frustration'. It will end with the last trumpet. The form of this universe will pass away. Human beings are not to aspire to *become* 'natural'. This is what they already are. To find salvation they must become more than they are.

To many of our contemporaries the possibility of transcending nature appears to be arrogance, a kind of 'species-ism'. Eco-feminists in particular have insisted that there is a close and damaging relationship between reductionist science and transcendental monotheism. That is the reason why many of them are hostile to Christianity. The arrogance of the human species begins with God's giving dominion to Adam over the natural world. Many New Age movements teach that what we need to do to be saved is to 'come home' to nature, to recognise our creatureliness, our co-dependence on the plant and animal creation. As expressions of the 'self-healing tautology' we are encouraged to express interdependence through an awakening of the senses, which might include such things as circle dancing, touch, silence, massage and aromatherapy. All these may play their part in healing the estranged self. There is an asceticism which belongs to these fashionable new theologies. There is a fear of certain foods or of food in general. Just as the planet has been poisoned, so have many foodstuffs and the air we breathe. There is an investment in the streamlined androgynous body, male in its hardness and slimness, female in its prettiness. What is the significance of these fashions and fads? Surely they are techniques for overcoming the sense of separateness. They are attempts to overcome estrangement between the self and nature and between the genders. Salvation is given in the moment that separateness is overcome. This is direct knowledge of the interconnected self which is also knowledge of God.

New Age belief systems have been compared with Gnosticism. It is true that they share with Gnosticism a fascination with cosmology and psychology, swinging between permissiveness and asceticism. Yet they differ from Gnosticism in their central attitude to nature. For Gnosticism creation *was* the Fall. Salvation lay in escape

155

from the body, in a dramatic passage through the aeons to reunion with the divine. There was a vivid drama attached to the soul's flight from this world.

Contemporary creation-centred spirituality has no such escape route. This world is all there is. And it is here that creation spirituality runs itself into the ground. For in spite of Matthew Fox's insistence on replacing original sin with original blessing, it is not clear that this strategy actually speaks to the real anxiety hovering over the human race. We do not feel very blessed. In fact we fear that we are killing our world. We are destroying the very web which gives us life and a future. What is far more likely and is more rarely expressed is that the web that gives us life could find ways of destroying us. Yet this is what Bateson suggests, calmly, and without anxiety. Either way, behind all the positive, celebratory, life-affirming rhetoric of the creation and New Age theologies is a layer of anxious guilt, which can neither be confessed nor healed. The terror is that we really have screwed it up, corporately and on a cosmic scale. The fear of ecological disaster is worse than the fear that we would destroy ourselves in a nuclear holocaust. At least nuclear destruction was something we could blame on aspects of ourselves that we know about. Human violence and aggression are familiar evils. But the destruction of nature has come about as much through our creativity and ingenuity as through our wickedness. And whereas the decision to embark on a nuclear war was one that would be taken or not by named and accountable individuals, the degradation of our environment is a shared responsibility.

In the light of this potentially cosmic loss, individual death has paled into insignificance. It is not seen in quite the tragic way that it was in Monod's world. Tragedy there is, of course, for mourners, but I am struck by the lack of anxiety that many of my contemporaries seem to feel about the annihilation of the self at death. They do not expect an afterlife and seem unanxious about it. Death has almost become a resolution, a way of overcoming estrangement, of achieving unity through personal unconsciousness. Perhaps these days oblivion is desired rather than feared.

Religion has always offered a way of salvation from our personal and cosmic dilemmas. But now the offers appear to have run out. If there is nowhere else to go and this world is all, we have a grim choice. Either we ignore the problems of our environment and carry on despoiling the earth until doomsday, or we give our lives to communal protest, campaigns, vigils and so forth in the knowledge that all our efforts may prove to be of no avail. The consequence of this dilemma is that any kind of religious commitment is insincere. How can we pray and worship God when we are soiled with a guilt so deep that it cannot be accessed, let alone healed? One might go further and suggest that any kind of *commitment* seems insincere. If the world is dying, and there is no God outside the world, the self has no meaning. Cosmic pessimism is linked, at least in the Western world, to a new economic insecurity, which brings an incalculable weight of stress and anxiety. The individual self is simply not strong enough to bear the weight of hope. Post-modern drift is a way of life, with fewer people feeling confident enough to marry or to put down roots, let alone to belong to or join any meaning-bearing community. The best we can hope for is to gather nuggets of wisdom, like autumn squirrels hoarding nuts. We find ourselves in a pick and mix world, in which nature has declared we are no longer welcome. This rejection of our humanity by the environment which bears us makes orphans of us all. We *cannot* make community because the cosmic grounds for trusting each other have been removed. All religion can do is to offer therapy and techniques of spiritual self-management, and neither the therapy nor the techniques are to be trusted if they come with big ideas or ideals. These are limited goals which may help to lessen the pain of existence. No more is expected or desired. Even within the Church patterns of commitment seem looser and more fragile. It is no big deal to drift in or out of Church life without losing, or gaining any particular faith.

The problem, of course, is that Christianity has lost confidence in its foundations, in the reality of God as distinct from this world. Creation theology is no substitute for a rational theology of creation. Of course, there have been

157

times in Christian history when the distance of God from this world was too sharply drawn. We know the distortions which could follow, a ghoulish obsession with death, an over-concern about hell and heaven, and a grim indifference to matters of justice on earth. But in our age we seem to have lost any sense of 'otherness' at all. We have incorporated the secular agenda so thoroughly that we no longer know how to conceive of Christianity except in terms of what it contributes to the enhancement of human life on earth. What we have lost is any sense of our faith as containing a sure and certain hope of a life greater than this one, in which both soul and body are contained. Human life on earth was never intended to be the end of the matter.

In fact the two moods towards nature which I have outlined, far from setting the only framework in which Christianity can operate, set up intolerable anxieties in the human spirit, which only a restoration of transcendence can heal. To ascribe to the world an absolute value is to put a strain on the self which few of us can bear. We know we cannot cope with the heroic expectations of Monod and Cox; but nor can we bear the fragmentation which comes from our more recent sense of being too closely connected to everything else. We might ponder on why we find both heroism and fragmentation so unbearable. Could it be that there is that within the human spirit which is incomplete without a recognition that its true destiny lies beyond this world? That still hears the call from further on and further in? In orthodox Christianity a proper attitude of care towards the self, the neighbour and nature does not arise from the terror that all will be taken away. Such terror leads only to moral paralysis, the precise inability to act or suffer authentically that seems to grip our secularised world. Monod's dream of ethical scientific socialism has not survived the collapse of Communism. Bateson's concern for the wholeness of things requires a wholly other if it is not to fragment into narcissism. We need to reassert the argument that care and concern arise from the fact that the self, the neighbour and the world have relative, rather than absolute value. They are valuable because they are valued by God.

Lady Julian's hazelnut image comes to mind: 'It is, because God loves it.'

The most important task for those who hope to see a robust Christian tradition available for the next millenium is to reconstruct a Christian theory of knowledge, which would enable us to interpret the insights of contemporary science without incorporating its despair or indifference. Such a theory of knowledge would need to build on the sheer graciousness of existence, arguing that it is a primal miracle that there is anything here at all. The response to the fact of existence is not anxiety, or even in the first instance, curiosity, but praise. The Church, by its free offering of worship witnesses to the limits of chance and necessity as explanations of our universe.

Second, it would need to build on the remarkable fact that our minds have evolved in such a way as to understand our universe. This breathtaking truth is sometimes dismissed, but the way it is dismissed is revealing. Stephen Hawking, for example, speaks of human beings as though we are innocent winners of a cosmic horse race looking back to the starting line and assuming that we must have been special to win. No, he insists, we just happen to be the lucky ones. *Happen* to be? Is that really likely? Christian apologists have been slow to expose these sleights of hand. It is simply incomprehensible that we should comprehend, unless we are set in a framework of meaning. The congruence of our minds with how things are is the basis for understanding the human vocation as a priestly one; we are here to articulate the praises and prayers of our universe.

Third, it must build on the historic revelation of God's nature through oral and written tradition, taking account of the fact that in a multi-faith world, to acknowledge particular disclosures in one set of historically conditioned writings need not exclude the possibility of such disclosures in others. The tension one finds in the world's scriptures between the unknowability of God and his accessibility and intimacy is evidence of universal human experience.

And fourth, the instinct of mysticism, which does not die in spiritually thin times like our own, even when it has to

159

drink from polluted wells, should remind us of the urgent need to formulate a rational faith, based in a theistic cosmology, which speaks to the heart as well as to the mind. None of these agendas is new, of course, but they have been much neglected in recent years. The reason people abandon Christianity is that they assume, often rightly, that we have nothing to offer that they do not already know about.

Notes to Chapter 7

1 *Chance and Necessity* (Fount Paperbacks, 1977) (originally published in France in 1970 under the title *Le hasard et la necessité*).
2 Chandler Publishing Company, 1972.
3 Fontana, 1980.
4 Pelican, 1968.

8 Against Anxiety, Beyond Triumphalism: Christians and Religious Diversity[1]

Philip Lewis

The Lambeth Conference in 1988 commended dialogue with people of other faiths as part of Christian discipleship and mission. Such a task has assumed an even greater urgency with the collapse of Communism. The demise of a bi-polar world of superpower politics has seen a proliferation of religious and ethnic conflicts. However, for many Christians inter-religious understanding remains peripheral to their concerns. The need to remedy this situation has become a priority. In a lecture to Muslim scholars at Al-Azhar University in Cairo in October 1995 Dr George Carey, the Archbishop of Canterbury, remarked: 'It is extraordinary how ignorant we are of one another. Yet ignorance is the most terrible of cultural diseases for from it stem fear, misunderstanding and intolerance.' The Archbishop went on to repeat a hope he had voiced in a lecture delivered earlier in the year in Madras: 'I long for the day when all those studying their own faith in depth will also be required to examine the life and teachings of two other faiths as well.'[2]

Such views are, in part, a response to one of the most significant aspects of social change in Britain since the Second World War: the creation and consolidation of Muslim, Sikh and Hindu communities, part of that larger flow of migrants from former British colonies invited to fill the labour shortages in the fifties and sixties. Britain's new religious minorities vary in size and socio-economic profile. Extrapolations from the 1991 census suggest that Hindus

161

number 400,000, Muslims 1 million (75 per cent of whom originate from South Asia) and Sikhs 400,000. This contrasts with Britain's oldest religious minority, the Jews, who number 300,000. Demographic projections indicate that by 2011 Hindu and Sikh communities will increase to half a million each while Muslims will probably double.

These communities are overwhelmingly concentrated in urban areas, and most especially in London, the industrial cities of the Midlands, and the textile towns of Yorkshire and Lancashire. Each city has a different mix of communities; Wolverhampton has a majority of Sikhs, Leicester a majority of Hindus and Bradford a majority of Muslims. Bradford exemplifies just how recent the formation of such communities has been. In 1961 the ethnic minority component of the population was 4,000, in 1991 77,000. This figure is projected to increase to 140,000 in 2011, some 110,000 of whom will be Muslims, or one fifth of the residents in the Metropolitan District.

The 'Asian' communities have different socio-economic trajectories, with the Hindus and Sikhs outperforming the ethnic majority on most indicators, while the Bangladeshi Muslims are languishing far behind all other communities, in part because they entered Britain last, at a time of rapid restructuring and recession in the national economy. As with wider society, Pakistani and Bangladeshi communities are increasingly polarised into those who are economically successful and those at the very base of the social pyramid whose lot has worsened. Most worrying for the future are statistics of educational disadvantage:

> While a third of all 16–24 year olds in 1988–1990 had a GCE A-level or equivalent or higher qualifications, only 18 per cent of Pakistanis and 5 per cent of Bangladeshis did. Moreover these two minorities were the only ones to be significantly out of line with the findings that overall 20 per cent of this age group had no qualifications whatever. The proportion of Pakistanis and Bangladeshi 16–24 year olds with no qualifications was 48 and 54 per cent respectively.[3]

The emergence of British Muslim, Hindu and Sikh communities has happened at a time when political and social scientists have belatedly awoken to the fact of a renewed significance of religion world-wide, not least in public life. To make sense of this development, the phrase 'religious nationalism' has been coined – far more useful for description and comparative analysis than the term 'fundamentalism', with its pejorative baggage. In all, a growing number of studies challenge the adequacy of the secularisation thesis which presupposed the increasing marginalisation of religion across the world in the wake of modernisation.[4]

Further, with developments in communications technology, transport and information, which bring events in distant parts of the world within easy reach – the process of globalisation – it is no longer enough to understand contextualised, local expressions of the world's religions. Each has to be located within such a global perspective. In December 1992 Hindu religious nationalists destroyed a mosque at Ayodhya in India with the active financial support of diaspora communities which had blessed and sent bricks with which to build a new temple on the same site. Within days Hindu temples and properties were attacked in Britain. It is hardly surprising that Professor John Bowker in a recent book introduces the section on religion with the question, 'Why are religions so dangerous?' and insists that understanding religious commitment and its organisation is every bit as urgent as ecology and environmental studies.[5]

I want in this chapter to do three things. Firstly, to underline the complexity and difficulty of inter-religious and inter-communal encounter in England today. To do this I shall sketch some of the changing priorities of two other religious communities as they also struggle with issues of tradition and change. Secondly, I want to identify and justify some of the public and civic responsibilities which churches carry in English society and to ask what resources they have to draw on in seeking to discharge these in a context of religious plurality. Finally, I want to spell out some of the intellectual and spiritual tasks facing the churches if they are to transmit and embody the Christian tradition in a new situation and to offer some personal reflections on what this might involve.

I wish first to consider the situation facing the Anglo-Jewish communities, the oldest religious minority, and then one of the newer religious minorities, British Muslims. Anglo-Jewry provides a window into the perplexities of sustaining a separate religious identity within an open society which exercises a strong assimilationist appeal. In the 1950s Jewish communities numbered 450,000, in the 1990s 300,000. The stigma against marrying out is much diminished. In an article in the *Jewish Chronicle* entitled 'Have we failed the challenge of freedom?' the Chief Rabbi, Jonathan Sacks, lamented that:

> Throughout the diaspora, one young Jew in two is deciding not to marry another Jew ... The most pressing question each of us must face is: Will we have Jewish grandchildren? ... Ask a Jew in the diaspora what is the most powerful reminder that he or she is a Jew, and the answer will be – anti-Semitism. It is as if we still see Jewish identity as a prison constructed out of other people's prejudice.[6]

The reasons for this parlous situation are many and controversial. Reform Jews consider contemporary Orthodoxy seriously dysfunctional, with the majority not conforming to the dictates of legal (*halakhic*) observance and viewing the bulk of rituals and observances as anachronistic and burdensome.[7] Many Jews, traumatised by the holocaust, abandoned belief in God and substituted Israel as the way of affirming their Jewishness. However, while Israel retains a central place in Jewish loyalties, it too has become the location of controversy and disillusion. It has been estimated that some half a million Jews have left Israel, the majority of whom were secular. Lord Jakobovits, the previous Chief Rabbi, in a recent study launched a scathing indictment of the 'bankruptcy' of the traditional Orthodox leadership in Israel, its separatism and rejection of the secular world, and its 'utter folly' in supporting Israel's invasion of Lebanon in 1982 – 'leaving it to the secularists to articulate the Jewish conscience and salvage the Jewish honour'; he went on to argue for the disestablishment of the Israeli rabbinate so that the forces of 'sane Judaism' might combine 'to curb the wave of neo-Khomeinistic fanaticism which threatens to engulf the Jewish world'.[8]

Lord Jakobovits' exasperation and anguish can, in part, be explained by two developments in recent Israeli history, which inevitably have an impact on Anglo-Jewry. Firstly, the vast expansion of numbers studying in *yeshivot*, traditional rabbinic seminaries. These seminaries, often based on Lithuanian models, include at best a minimalist secular curriculum, and make little attempt to teach a broad general culture, with the language of instruction often Yiddish rather than modern Hebrew. Since the *yeshiva* students are also exempt from military service, they have recreated a relatively closed world. With the founding of the State of Israel in 1948, David Ben-Gurion, the first prime minister, allowed some 400 students to defer military service indefinitely so as to replenish the store of talmudic scholarship decimated in the war. By the late 1980s the number of such exemptions had grown to 18,000. Such a process of socialisation and intellectual formation is unlikely to generate a religious leadership able to engage with the problems which exercise many of their co-religionists and fellow citizens.

This pattern of religious formation was until recently largely alien to the English situation. The premier training institute for Orthodox rabbis in England was Jews' College in London. Founded in 1879 to train rabbis, it was characterised by four features which ensured an educated religious leadership able to engage confidently with wider society: it taught in English, students were expected to get BAs from London University in secular subjects, it concentrated on classical fields of Jewish scholarship and saw itself as a centre of scholarly excellence contributing to the science of Judaism.[9] What is now clear is that Jews' College, which recently was threatened with closure, is having to compete with the products of more traditional *yeshivot*. One recent estimate suggested that about 50 per cent of Orthodox rabbis were now drawn from this world. This is a cause of concern and debate within Anglo-Jewry. A recent article in the *Jewish Chronicle* worried about this development, insisting that it was not 'an improvement to have rabbis with only the merest smattering of general education and an inbuilt bias against university qualifications, except where these are unavoidable in earning a living.'[10]

The second development which worries Lord Jakobovits has been the emergence since Israel's Six Day War in 1967 of a religious Zionism which is messianic. The stunning victory of 1967 gave Israel control of the West Bank and East Jerusalem. For the first time for almost two millenia Jews could pray freely at the wailing wall within a united Jerusalem. Biblical Judaea and Samaria were once again in Jewish hands. These victories were invested with religious significance by many outside the 15 per cent of Israelis who vote for the country's religious parties. By 1974, from within religious Zionism, *Gush Emunim* (the Bloc of the Faithful) had emerged, committed to settling and consolidating Israeli control of the occupied territories. Although never more than 20,000 strong, this movement captured the imagination of many in Israel. Its genuine pioneering spirit revived the cherished memory of the early Zionist settlers and their religious Zionism could be presented as the true heir of that most revered early tradition of settlement, self-sacrifice and self-defence. From 1977 to 1992 their activities were supported by the right-wing ruling party, Likud.

Along with the religious idealists came a dangerous brand of religious extremism, often funded and staffed by diaspora Judaism in America. Dr Baruch Goldstein, who massacred 30 Muslims at prayer in Hebron in March 1994, was affiliated to such groups, aptly descibed by Amos Oz, one of Israel's leading writers and peace activists, as 'Hizbollah in a skullcap'.[11] The tragedy of contemporary Israeli politics is that such religious nationalism, which has sacralised the land, has rendered the search for peace more intractable. The transfer of occupied land to the Palestinians in exchange for peace can be construed as an act of wilful disobedience to God's will. Indeed, in July 1995 a 1500-member organisation called the Rabbinical Council – headed by a former Chief Rabbi of Israel – decreed that any evacuation of Israeli military bases or settlements in the occupied territories would be contrary to Jewish law and thus prohibited.

Needless to say, Anglo-Jewry has been as divided as Israel on these issues. What seems to be happening is that Anglo-Jewry, no longer energised by immigration, increasingly distracted by assimilation and debates about Israel, is finding its inclusive brand of Orthodoxy – once described as the Anglican Establishment (Jewish Branch) – undercut by an increase in Reform and Progressive Judaism on the one hand, and ultra-Orthodoxy on the other. With this has gone an increasing intra-Jewish intolerance. The last word, however, should go to the present Chief Rabbi, who recently launched an ambitious and integrated programme of education under the slogan of 'Jewish continuity'. Dr Sacks is candid about the challenges which such a process confronts:

> We have paid a painful price for two centuries of alienation between Judaism and many of the finest Jewish minds. Halakhic scholarship has continued to thrive, but essential areas of Jewish thought remain in their infancy. We know the rules governing relationships between Jew and Jew, but *our understanding of relationships between Jew and non-Jew in a plural and interdependent world is far from clear* [emphasis mine]. Only recently have scholars begun to evolve Judaic responses to macro-economic, political, environmental and scientific questions.
>
> The consequence is that we have an artificially narrow sense of what constitutes a Jewish deed. We know that going to synagogue or keeping *kashrut* [dietary laws] is Jewish. Yet, we are not sure that there is a Judaic way of being an academic or a journalist or an artist or an architect or a politician. When Jews speak as Jews in the public arena, they often confuse Jewish self-interests (or the general interests of minorities) with Judaic principle. Nor, ironically, is it any different in Israel. There, the religious voice is identified with sectarian politics and sectional self-interest rather than societal ideals in the tradition of the prophets and the sages ... It is not true to say that living in two worlds has failed. It is fairer to say that it has not seriously been tried.[12]

To turn to Britain's Muslim communities is to notice both similarities and dissimilarities with the concerns evident within Anglo-Jewry. A main difference turns on the struc-

167

tural location of both communities: the Anglo-Jewish community today is largely drawn from the business and professional classes and is well represented in the political process, in the mainstream media and in civic and cultural life. By contrast, the largest Muslim communities, those from Pakistani backgrounds, can be characterised as 'a semi-industrialised, newly urbanised working class community ... only one generation away from rural peasantry'.[13] There are no Muslim MPs and very few Muslims in the media.

Traditionally, religious and ethnic minorities are only newsworthy if they can be presented as either a threat or victim. Muslims, in the wake of the *Satanic Verses* affair and the Gulf crisis, had few advocates and, thus, were routinely presented as 'fundamentalists' and potential subversives. The closest parallel in British history is the demonisation of Irish Catholic migrants in the middle and late nineteenth century. They too were largely migrants from rural backgrounds with little formal education and who spoke a foreign language. They were often blamed by the indigenous working class for depreciating wages. Antagonism to them was legitimised by anti-Catholic sentiment reaching back to the Reformation, with Roman Catholicism considered a synonym for superstition, moral corruption, intolerance and potential treason. For the Protestant and liberal imagination they were the significant 'other' in contrast with whom identity was defined. Across the political spectrum they were considered candidates for control and suppression.[14]

Another important difference between the Jews and Muslims is the fact that the latter are still in the process of community formation and consolidation amidst the dislocation, literal and metaphorical, of migration. An invaluable insight into this process is provided by Eva Hoffman's autobiography, *Lost in Translation*, and subtitled *A Life in a New Language*. Hoffman, a secular Jewess from Poland, writes of her experiences of having to leave Cracow in the early 1950s with her parents because of the recrudescence of anti-Semitism. She was in her early teens and bitterly resented the move to Canada. However, she soon mastered English and became an editor of the *New York Times Book Review.*

The first part of her title refers to her parents' experience, the second refers to her own. I want to rehearse a few of her comments which resonate with the experiences of many migrant communities in Britain. She remarks that the first generation of migrants are generally caught between nostalgia and alienation. The price of migration was to be cut off from part of your own story which was 'apt to veil it in a haze of nostalgia, which is an ineffectual relationship to the past, and the haze of alienation, which is an ineffectual relationship to the present.' Highly articulate and able herself, she soon recognised that linguistic competence enabled the migrant to overcome the stigma of marginality and thus be in a position to translate anger into argument. This she contrasted with the linguistic dispossession of many in the inner city of New York. When living there she would listen nightly to fights between different ethnic minorities that would 'erupt like brushfire . . . In their escalating fury of repetitious phrases . . . I hear not the pleasure of macho toughness but an infuriated beating against wordlessness, against the incapacity to make oneself understood.'

Although a secular Jewess herself, when confronted by anti-semitism in Poland she responded by affirming her dignity through defiance and affirmation of her Jewishness:

> I gradually came to understand that it is a matter of honor to affirm my Jewishness and to do so with my head held high. That's what it meant to be a Jew – a defiance of those dark and barbaric feelings [of anti-semitism]. Through that defiance one upholds human dignity . . . It seems a simple affirmation of justice, of rightness, of reason that Jews are human the way other people are human.

This is the phenomenon sociologists describe as reactive identity. In Canada, Hoffman and her sister were also exposed to a variety of different ways of being Jewish, which often seemed outlandish and bewildering to her parents. Nonetheless, her parents stopped trying to influence them. She writes of her mother complaining that 'in

Poland, I would have known what to do', but in Canada she has lost her sureness of touch, her authority. Finally, she notes that her Canadian friends were 'more generous toward me than I was toward them; but then, a sense of disadvantage and inferiority is not a position from which one can feel the largeheartedness of true generosity.'[15]

Hoffman's insights illuminate many of the dilemmas of Britain's Muslims. Most are located within inner city areas within relatively encapsulated communities. I want here to illuminate two issues. First, to offer a brief profile of the diversity of expression evident amongst British Muslims as a corrective to the notion of Islam as a unitary phenomenon. Secondly, the predicament of a religious leadership, which finds it difficult to connect with many British-born and educated Muslims, still less with wider society.

The term 'fundamentalism' is now part of the journalist's lexicon in speaking of Islam. I have already made clear that I feel such a term as 'religious nationalism' is more useful. 'Fundamentalism' presupposes a unitary notion of Islam, spawning militant activists across the world, which obscures the diversity of traditions and groupings within Islam. It assumes that Muslims invariably march to the drum of an Ayatollah or an Iraqi dictator. It foreshortens 1400 years of Muslim history, assuming that Middle Eastern, Iranian and South Asian Muslims are identical. The reality is that no one is Muslim-in-general, floating free of culture-specific histories, notwithstanding a family resemblance in belief and custom across cultures.

Since the majority of Muslims in Britain are South Asian by descent, their understanding and practice of Islam bears that particular impress. Historically, Islam was rooted in the hearts and minds of South Asians by dynasties of *sufis* – 'friends of God' – revered as mediators between man and God, considered bearers of God's blessing and healing. Their tombs became an accessible and alternative focus for pilgrimage for the majority who could never afford to make the *hajj* to Mecca and Madina. The *sufis* and their devotees generated a rich vernacular tradition of devotional hymns. These religious songs – *qawwalis* – have given consolation and delight to Muslims for more than 600 years, not least for their criticism of bookish, but stone-hearted religious scholars, *ulama*, who are pilloried for knowing nothing of love. The *sufis* were the creators and custodians of regional languages and cultures. Their shrines were a key element in the gradual Islamisation of South Asian peoples.

Alongside this tradition of saints and shrines, the trauma of colonialism generated a range of responses: an apolitical revivalism, rejecting Western intellectual and cultural influences, and seeking to create self-contained communities with an isolationist ethos; an Islamic modernism, which sought to remain faithful to the Islamic tradition, yet open to an honest engagement with the West – this tradition is now on the defensive world-wide but its main bearers today tend to be Muslim women's movements; 'Islamism', a religio-political movement, presenting Islam as an all-encompassing ideology, seeking to capture political power in Muslim majority areas. Among intellectuals a progressive writers' movement emerged, which looked critically at the abuses of religious and political leadership and was concerned with social and economic reform. All these expressions of Muslim religion and culture have been transplanted into Britain. However, since the majority of settlers came from the least developed areas of South Asia, modernism, Islamism and similar urban phenomena have been slow to take root.[16]

The products of traditional Islamic seminaries which provide religious leadership in the mosques – the *ulama* – are increasingly out of their depth in British society. An Indian *imam*, who has served his community for many years in Britain, recently offered a candid analysis of the difficulties facing them. He contends that mosques have been turned into 'medieval sectarian fortresses' and painted a bleak picture of his fellow *ulama*:

> The majority ... lack a thorough knowledge of Islam. Their knowledge is limited to the sectarian parameters ... [they] do not know anything about the context in which they are resident. They can neither speak the English language nor are they acquainted with the socio-political context of the dominating

171

British culture ... [the *imam*] is dogmatic or does not know how to reason.[17]

Little wonder that Dr Shabbir Akhtar, a member of the Bradford Council for Mosques, observed that 'traditional Islam is in sorry decline; many in the educated classes are repelled by it. By refusing to address the problems that plague the modern mind ... Islam is gradually losing control ... over the daily life of secularised believers.' To address the situation Akhtar argues that it is imperative to develop 'a critical koranic scholarship' and 'a natural theology, responsive to the intellectual pressures and assumptions of a sceptical age, which could be used to remove some kinds of conscientious doubts about the truth of religious claims.'[18]

It is hardly surprising that the majority of *ulama* are unable to connect with the world of young British Muslims. Throughout the 1980s and 1990s a hybrid Muslim youth culture was emerging, enjoying social space and a measure of freedom in schools, colleges, youth and community centres. A large part of this culture turns on music, often a combination of bhangra and reggae, alien and inaccessible to many of the elders. Many of these youngsters were the first in their families to enjoy formal education. Unlike their parents, they were at ease with British society and street-wise. This has created major problems for the transmission of an informed understanding of Islam across the generations. Gender is another area of contention, with many educated women not prepared to follow village customs and ready to challenge male hegemony.

While traditional Islam is increasingly inaccessible to a new generation of British Muslims, this does not mean that they have turned their back on Islam. Their religion often functions as part of a reactive identity, whereby they counter wider society's racism and phobia about Islam. Their Islam is very much a do-it-youself variety, culled from such pamphlets or books available in English. At best, this is a haphazard introduction to the riches of the Islamic tradition, lacking the disciplines and methodology of traditional scholarship. At worst, such works as are available are either polemical diatribes against the West or simplistic appeals to return to the sources of Islam, which discount 1500 years of history and disciplined reflection.

The literature of such radical groups active in Britain as *Hizb at-Tahrir*, the Party of Liberation, falls within this category of anti-Western rhetoric. The movement was founded in Palestine in the 1950s as a splinter group within the Muslim Brotherhood. It is commited to the recreation of the Caliphate, abolished in 1924 by the Turkish leader, Mustafa Kemal. Banned across the Arab world, its agenda is not immediately relevant to British Muslims. It serves to exemplify Hoffman's point about new expressions of religiosity available for the sons and daughters of migrants with which to experiment, often to the dismay and bewilderment of parents. The leadership, dynamics and ethos of such groups has been vividly and sympathetically drawn in Hanif Kureishi's recent novel, *The Black Album*. In the figure of Riaz, the student leader, Kureishi captures and communicates their appeal to some disaffected British Muslim students. Riaz's Sunday talks in the mosque

> were well attended by a growing audience of young people, mostly local . . . Asians. Not being an aged obscurantist, Riaz was becoming the most popular speaker . . . He entitled his talks, 'Rave from the Grave?', 'Adam and Eve not Adam and Steve', 'Islam: A Blast from the Past or a Force for the Future?' and 'Democracy is a Hypocrisy'.[19]

However, it would be wrong to suggest that the generality of British Muslims have embraced radical Islam, with its casual anti-Semitism and homophobia. More pressing a worry for many parents and religious leaders is that because the religious tradition is inaccessible to many youngsters, beyond the minimalist diet to which many are exposed in the mosque, Islam becomes at best one component in their cultural identity, a condition of community belonging, inescapable but of declining relevance.

If the challenge to contemporary Judaism, at least in Israel, is to adjust to power after two millenia of relative powerlessness, the problem for Muslim minorities is the exact opposite. Dr Zaki Badawi, the distinguished Egyptian scholar, and former Director of the prestigious Islamic Cultural Centre and Mosque in London, has repeatedly remarked that the dilemma of Muslims in the West is exacerbated because Muslim theology offers no systematic formulation of the status of being in a minority. Muslims from Pakistan and Bangladesh migrated from Muslim-majority nations where state power and law were supportive of Islam. The situation in Britain, where the state is at best neutral and the law only marginally responsive to Islamic customs, has created a totally new and unfamiliar situation for them.

Thus far I have treated religious communities in isolation from each other. If we now ask about the relationship of British Jews and Muslims it is clear that they are still embryonic. Firstly, for reasons of geography Muslim and Jewish communities do not physically interact in many places. The majority of Anglo-Jewry live in London and southern suburban England. The majority of Muslims live outside London and in the inner-city areas of many cities. Such meeting as occurs in London tends to be conflictual, with Jewish students on London campuses protesting against the radical and anti-Semitic rhetoric of groups such as *Hizb at-Tahrir*. There is the possibility for constructive meeting in such cities as Leeds and Manchester, especially with the emergence of a Muslim professional and business sector.

There are individuals in both communities urging the need to develop contacts, especially with the re-emergence of xenophobia and anti-Semitism across Europe. However, attitudes generally appear to be marked by ambivalence or antagonism. This is clear in the 1994 review by the Runnymede Commission on Antisemitism, *A Very Light Sleeper: the persistence and dangers of antisemitism*. In addressing such important issues it is clear that inter-religious and inter-communal tension cannot be side-stepped. This is the burden of argument in an article by the director of the Jewish Council for Racial Equality, Edie Friedman, where she frankly acknowledges that

The relationship between Jews and Muslims is [a] fraught area.

The nettle to be seized here is to acknowledge the tensions between us at the same time as working together to foster Muslim-Jewish dialogue on a community – and not simply inter-faith – level. There is considerable anti-Muslim and anti-Jewish feeling in our society, and our best hope of reducing this is to work together to help change this climate to a more relaxed and generous one, enabling us the freedom to satisfy our religious needs, for example with regard to shechitah and halal. This requires our two communities themselves to adopt a more relaxed and generous attitude toward one another.[20]

What now of Christian responsibilities and the resources they can draw on, as they seek to respond to this complex and confused situation of religious plurality today? Churches as institutions and Christians generally have inherited a range of public and civic roles. This is neither surprising nor to be regretted: over six million Christians continue to worship regularly and some 65 per cent of British people affirm a loose Christian affiliation. Christians confronted with the demands of truth in worship and called to be 'moral communities' continue to be dispro-portionately found crossing new frontiers in care and service.[21] Churches have generated or contributed to that dense network of associations and voluntary organisations which cumulatively amount to one of the glories of Western culture – civil society.

In Britain civil society includes civic religion: chaplaincies to Parliament, Lord Mayors, the armed forces, universities, industry, and wherever people are vulnerable, whether hospitals or prisons. Public service broadcasting continues to include religion, with audience figures for *Songs of Praise* exceeding those of *Match of the Day*.[22] Tax payers continue to fund theology departments, which means that the discipline is not ghettoised into confessional colleges. It can continue its dialogue with academic life in all its diversity, and act as a brake on irrational and intolerant expressions of Christianity. Professor Adrian Hastings has recently argued that the great strength of the religious scene in Britain is that an Anglican establishment has been pluralised to make public space for other Christian denominations without in the process being privatised:

> Today Christian Aid, the Catholic Institute of International Relations, and ever so many other bodies and individuals from Frank Field to the Bishop of Oxford, all represent differing faces of the Church vis a vis the state and public political life . . . [with] the establishment still there to assert constitutionally, publicly and symbolically the church's relevance both to public policy and to the care of the most needy.[23]

It is vital to stress this point of Christianity pluralised as a necessary safeguard against a dangerous nostalgia in some Christian circles on the political right for unitary notions of Church and State, a Christian variant of what I have called religious nationalism.

In fact, because public and civic life is permeated with Christian influence it is proving increasingly hospitable to religious diversity: Radio Four's early morning *Thought for the Day* includes contributions from a number of Britain's faith communities. Many departments of theology have been pluralised to include religious studies. Hospital and prison chaplains are beginning to respond to the pastoral needs of all religious communities. New local agreed religious education syllabi, while reflecting the predominant influence of Christianity on English history, culture and institutions, also have to make space for Britain's new religious traditions. Agreed model syllabi for religious education have been drawn up by members of the different religions themselves. The Department of the Environment set up the Inner Cities Religious Council in 1992, which has sought to work in partnership with all the faith communities at local and national levels on the regeneration of inner cities and deprived outer estates. Because Christians and Jews enjoy voluntary-aided (VA) status for their schools, Muslims are in position to press for their own on the back of an equal opportunities' agenda, without being seen to be pressing for a privileged status – unlike the situation they face in republican and laicised France. Anglican and Catholic hierarchies have often supported Muslims in this regard. The Catholic Bishop of Leeds, the hierarchy's specialist on education, in supporting local Muslims in their bid for VA status, pointedly remarked:

> The experience of my own community, which has been a persecuted minority, is that having our own schools within the state system helped us to move out of our initial isolation, so as to become more confident and self-assured. The effect of separate schools for us has been integration, not divisiveness.[24]

Dr Tariq Modood, in an important and much-quoted article, argues that the real threat to minority faiths comes not from an Established Church but from 'a virtually unchallengeable and culturally insensitive secular centre which makes demands on all faiths, but especially on the least Westernised faiths at a time when the minority faiths are asserting themselves as a form of cultural defence.' He is surely right to insist that 'to devalue and marginalise religion in public life' would further reduce religious minorities to second-class status. The Established Church is given cautious support as offering 'some slight counterweight to the secular hegemony and . . . [any] proposals to dismantle establishment in the name of multi-faithism must be viewed as disingenuous.'[25]

Dr Sacks, in his 1990 Reith lectures, also supported a public role for Christianity. In his lectures he worried about religious and ideological diversity toppling over into tribalism. If this was to be avoided, Sacks urged the need for all to become 'bilingual': all must learn a first and public language of citizenship to enable all to live together. Alongside this first language is our second language, learned in family, community and its attendant institutions, religious or secular. The first language could not simply be a list of abstract rights but a national culture, even where that 'language' has been shaped by the ethos of the dominant group. Thus the Chief Rabbi argued against disestablishment, since this would represent 'a significant retreat from the notion that we share any values and beliefs at all'.[26]

The churches themselves are aware that they have a responsibility to use their institutional influence to enable a dialogue with other religious communities. Leaders of the

Church of England and the Church of Scotland recently articulated their responsibilities as national churches thus:

> to hold in trust the nation's religious commitment, i.e. its recognition of the place and importance of religion and religious freedom; secondly, to discover a language in which society may discuss itself in transcendental terms and agree on common values to inform its public ethics and policies.[27]

This careful formulation neither assumes the existence of universal moral norms shared by all religions nor does it gloss over the possibility of profound disagreements. Wisely, it neither assumes in advance of any conversation where such disagreements are to be located nor dramatises the incompatibility of such values. This commitment to patient conversation with other traditions in a shared search to envisage and embody the common good acts as a check on churches becoming just one more interest-group in competition for benefits and power in rivalry with others. If society is not to fragment further intellectually, culturally and morally, it is vital that churches do not evade such public responsibilities. This presupposes that churches do not endorse the fashionable relativism of post-modernism, with its scepticism about the existence of truth, objective values and the impossibility of arriving at any agreed understanding by rational means. To travel this path is to trigger a crisis in public life with public discourse trivialised as amounting to little more than an exercise in assertion rather than discussion, propaganda rather than persuasion, where power alone rules.[28]

Granted the importance of such a public role, what resources can the churches draw on to develop the confidence to relate to other religious communities? Three might be singled out. First, Black and Asian Christians in Britain are an often overlooked asset. They have already challenged the churches to address issues of racism and racial exclusion, both within church life and wider society.[29] This is clearly a precondition for any honest engagement with many religious and ethnic minority communities. Many share a great deal of common culture with Muslims, Hindus and Sikhs. Since they are frequently bi-lingual and bi-cultural they can interpret and explain what is unfamiliar. As churches learn to welcome, appreciate and involve Black and Asian Christians, not least in positions of influence, so they become signs of hope to wider society as they embody in their own life something of the country's ethnic and cultural variety. It was significant that the ethnic minority press – as well as the mainstream media – took a keen interest in Bishop Michael Nazir Ali's appointment as the Anglican diocesan Bishop of Rochester.

Ethnic and cultural diversity within British churches is a reminder that they belong to world-wide communions, possessed of a broader perspective than nationalism encompasses. This transnational dimension of church life is a second important resource for Christians seeking to relate to religious minorities. It can act as an antidote to a Little Englander sentiment, which favours narrow and exclusive definitions of national identity. In all, churches have a vital contribution to make in the debate as to what is to count today as 'a British way of life'. Such a debate is long overdue. The historian Michael Howard has provocatively urged the need to reclaim and celebrate.

> the idea that British culture is not only distinctive but *properly* distinctive, something with its own value and legitimacy ... [since] the growth of an internationally-minded 'overclass' with their credit cards, overseas business contacts and holidays abroad, the growing internationalization of their cities, and increased provision for servicing tourism, all combine to leave behind a semi-educated and resentful underclass which defiantly takes as its symbols the national flag abandoned by the elites ... and displays them on new and less glorious battlefields. These debased relics of national identity are often all they have left of their self-respect.[30]

This issue of self-respect, or what has been dubbed the politics of recognition, is clearly not simply a concern of religious minorities. Modern society has eroded social hierarchies, where status and 'honour' were relatively fixed, in favour of the rhetoric of equality and human 'dignity'. Thus democracies have ushered in a politics of equal recognition, with a diversity of groups, cultures, special interests now

179

clamouring for equal status and public recognition of their identity. In this context, the white 'underclass' are either treated with scorn or simply ignored. One of the many strengths of the essays and reflections which comprise *God in the City* – the fruit of four years' work by the Archbishop of Canterbury's urban theology group – is that it renders these communities visible and gives them a voice.[31]

Concerned by the increasing signs of social fragmentation, a political scientist has powerfully argued the need for an inclusive British national identity, which he feels would contribute to restoring a sense of social solidarity and moral obligation across communities. A national identity

> helps to locate us in the world; it must tell us who we are, where we have come from, what we have done. It must . . . involve an essentially historical understanding, in which the present generation are seen as heirs to a tradition which they pass on to their successors. Of course the story is continually being written; each generation revises the past as it comes to terms with the problem of the present.[32]

Such an aspiration is one which the churches should respect. Without a history and story there is very little that we can say about ourselves. The story the churches tell is an integral part of such a national history and offers a critical purchase on it. By virtue of their transnational loyalties and multi-ethnic membership the churches can enable that story to be inclusive and help create the space for it to be open to imaginative reappropriation and extension by new religious communities.

The history of world mission and the experience of Christians who have worked across religious and cultural boundaries is a third major resource for contemporary inter-religious encounter. Kenneth Cracknell – the first full-time secretary in 1978 of the BCC's newly established Committee for Relations with People of Other Faiths – has put us all in his debt with his pioneering study of theological and missionary engagement with world religions between 1864 and 1914. The book, with its splendid title, *Justice, Courtesy and Love*, indicates how much contemporary

180

reflection on other faiths was anticipated by such pioneers.[33] If we are to respond to the challenges of inter-religious meeting we cannot afford to lapse into forgetfulness of such a crucial component in Christian tradition.

The history of Christian missions also illuminates how the Christian tradition is itself transformed in its journey across cultural and linguistic barriers. An excellent example is the Old Testament scholarship of John William Colenso (1814–83), the first Anglican Bishop of Natal, who raised questions about the historical character of parts of the Pentateuch. As his biographer reminds us:

> he undertook his Old Testament work because Zulus asked him why their own legends were to be regarded as heathen and bloodthirsty when so much of the biblical narrative was of exactly the same kind. So it was said that the bishop, who had gone to convert the Zulus, had himself been converted by them.[34]

An interesting and relevant footnote to Colenso's scholarly endeavours is that his work was one of the stimuli which provoked the Indian Muslim scholar, Sayyid Ahmad Khan (1817–98), to consider the sources of Islam within a critical historiographical perspective. Religious communities, cultures and nations are not windowless boxes, impermeable to each other.

So far I have reviewed some of the resources to enable and equip the churches to sustain a variety of public and civic roles in the context of religious plurality. My stress has been on the practical and ethical dimensions of Christian responsibility as it seeks for a measure of agreement on issues of rationality, justice and the common good which can command general support across a diversity of communities. The alternative is for each competing interest group – political, religious, class, ethnic – to generate 'its own *internal* criteria of supposed rationality in order to serve its own power-interests, [whereby] rational debate collapses . . . into *accusation, blame, corporate self-righteousness and conflict.*'[35] This public role already presupposes certain Christian convictions, and it is these I wish to render explicit, as well as expanding on some of the intellectual

181

and spiritual tasks specific to any serious inter-religious and inter-communal encounter in the present context.

The churches can evade a public role in two ways. They can retreat into 'a relaxed pluralism of privacies', but at the price of renouncing 'all authentic claims to truth and publicness'; or 'into the righteous purity of a siege mentality where [they] alone possess the truth ... [untroubled by] a messy pluralism ... In their comfortable isolation, they can ignore all the truths disclosed in the classics of other religions and secular cultures.'[36] It is apparent that I do not believe that either the 'pluralist' or 'exclusivist' option can adequately ground a responsible public role for the churches. However, it will be clear from the earlier discussion of world religions that inclusivist readings of the traditions are today being eroded by an 'exclusivism', itself often married to a public role best described as religious nationalism. I remain convinced that the trinitarian tradition contains the intellectual resources to avoid such dangers, enabling a concern for truth, undergirding a public role, while alert to what may be learned from the other. No one has formulated what I have in mind better than Rowan Williams in an essay on 'Trinity and Pluralism' where he insists that the church

> engages in dialogue and encounter to discover itself more truthfully, to put to other traditions the questions that arises from its own foundational story of Jesus ... nourished by the conviction that the story of Jesus and the Church, of logos and spirit manifest in the world, affords us a truthful vision of how God is – not exhaustive, not exclusive, but truthful.[37]

To say this is simply the first step in a costly engagement with the other. The Christian self-understanding so embodied is risked in encounter, individually and corporately, in personal and public life. It is analogous to what is referred to as pre-understanding in hermeneutics. It awaits confirmation, challenge, expansion or refinement through actual meeting. Inevitably, any serious engagement with religious traditions will involve a two-way challenge. Christians, especially those in the Protestant traditions, will be called to recover an understanding of the important community dimensions of all religions, including Christianity. This does not mean sentimentalising the notion of religious community, which can degenerate into an oppressive collectivity. Bishop John V. Taylor is surely right to insist that a corrosive individualism partly explains the eclipse of a sense of God for many in the West. Thus 'restoring the realities of genuine relationship', a rediscovery and embodiment of the biblical *koinonia*, remains a vital 'form of evangelism'.[38] Christians, for their part, are called to explain to Muslim and Hindu why the 'secular' is not simply to be dismissed as anti-religious.

In the Islamic or Hindu traditions the notion of the 'secular' is invariably construed as opposed to religion, and it is difficult to find a term to translate it in Hindi or Urdu which does not carry this connotation.[39] The New Testament, of course, displays an ambivalence to the 'secular'. This is captured in the phrase 'loving and hating the world' with which Wayne Meeks introduces a discussion of this in his splendid monograph, *The Origins of Christian Morality*.[40] This ambivalence is seen in St Augustine, who operated with the trichotomy of Christian (or sacred), secular (neutral, civic) and pagan (profane). The 'secular' – the Roman past embedded in the institutions and culture of contemporary society – for Augustine was to be evaluated in a Christian perspective in terms of the purposes it served. Robert Markus, in mapping the de-secularisation of Europe between Augustine (354–430) and Pope Gregory the Great (c. 540–604), is at pains to point out that 'Augustine's theology had carefully kept a space for an intermediate realm of the "secular" between the "sacred" and the "profane", his own inclinations ... were to defend this area from encroachment by the "sacred", from clerical interference and ecclesiastical dominance.'[41] The world of St Augustine seems closer to our own than that of Pope Gregory, which looks forward to medieval Christendom, in which the 'secular' has been turned into 'Christian' or dismissed as 'pagan'.

The Christian tradition cannot simply see itself as over against the 'secular'. Christians need to be alert to the real gains of the Enlightenment, notably tolerance and civil liberties. David Tracy is right to remind us that their corruptions are real enough, yet their corruptions 'pale beside the outright oppression inflicted by the self-righteous upon all those who will not share their univocal ideologies'.[42] The terrors of hell and the un-Christian maxim that 'conversion begins with fear' were similarly eroded through an alliance of innovative Christian thinkers and the satire of Voltaire and Diderot.

It will be clear that to transmit and embody Christianity in the context of religious diversity is an exacting and long-term project. To adapt the comment of the Chief Rabbi cited earlier, our understanding of the relationship between Christians and members of other religious communties in a plural and interdependent world is far from clear. Christians are no more immune than anyone else from the temptations of an exclusivism married to religious nationalism. Christians too are not Christians-in-general but shaped by a distinct history. I have argued that the public and civic responsibilities which British Christians have inherited are compatible with both the Christian claim to be bearers of truth and the shared task of searching for an understanding of the common good to which other people, religious and secular, can subscribe.

Christian tradition necessarily evolves in response to the challenges and opportunities of new ideas and circumstances, criticism from within and without, and past errors. Parts of our history better speak to our contemporary dilemmas than others. Therefore, I have argued that St Augustine's insistence on space for the 'secular' is particularly suggestive in our situation. The selective reappropriation of history and tradition must also include that creative encounter between theologians and missionaries encapsulated in the reports of the World Missionary Conference in Edinburgh in 1910. Thus, inter-faith relations can encourage a retrieval of forgotten dimensions of our own tradition. Historic Christianity also provides plenty of cul-de-sacs and dangerous distortions properly repented of and repudiated. Any inter-faith engagement helps us to be honest about the dark side of that history. If we are creatively to embody that multi-cultural and multi-ethnic diversity of contemporary Christianity – such a vital bridge in our engagement with other ethnic minorities and their faiths and cultures – there is need for penitence in the face of racial exclusion and the tardy welcome often extended to Black and Asian Christians.

Not only is Christianity a living tradition characterised by an evolving self-understanding of its central commitments but their precise meaning, content and implications are contested, as earlier chapters in this book have made abundantly clear. In seeking to develop a theology of religions, this diversity and disagreement is evident in the categories of exclusivism, pluralism and inclusivism in which most discussions are generally framed. In reality, on different issues one can move across categories. Thus, Bishop Lesslie Newbigin declares his own position to be

> exclusivist in the sense that it affirms the unique truth of the revelation of Jesus Christ, but it is not exclusivist in the sense of denying the possibility of the salvation of the non-Christian. It is inclusivist in the sense that it refuses to limit the saving grace of God to the members of the Christian Church, but it rejects the inclusivism which regards the non-Christian religions as vehicles of salvation. It is pluralist in the sense of acknowledging the gracious work of God in the lives of all human beings, but it rejects a pluralism which denies the uniqueness and decisiveness of what God has done in Jesus Christ.[43]

Such discussions are useful in so far as they enable a real meeting with members of other traditions. Whatever theological stance one adopts prior to such meeting, it cannot of itself pre-empt the need for discernment as one is called to make provisional theological and practical judgements within the context of extended encounter. Conflicts and disagreements are inevitable, but so long as they are the result of mutual understanding – the presupposition of genuine disagreement! – and have also identified some commonalities across traditions, then the effort has been worthwhile. However, we need to be aware that any genuine meeting with another is a good deal more exacting than most of us assume. The particularity and otherness of diverse religious traditions can threaten our own self-understanding and identity. The achievement of genuine mutuality and understanding is precarious and hostage to unforeseen contingencies.

I want to conclude with some summary observations which have informed my own inter-faith ministry and may resonate with the experiences of fellow practitioners. They do not amount to a theology of other religions but might find a place in such a quest. As with the UPA experience, which forms the context for discerning *God in the City*, the reality of inter-religious relations is too 'intractable, fragmented and contradictory' to be worked into a systematic theology.[44] First, there is a need to develop a place for honest perplexity in inter-religious meeting. I have long treasured St Paul's words in 2 Corinthians 4:8 where he speaks of being 'perplexed but not . . . driven to despair'. Karl Rahner devotes a chapter in his *Theological Investigations* to this verse, where he insists that perplexity is 'a feature of Christian life always and everywhere'.[45] One might see Romans 9–11 as Paul struggling with his perplexity over Israel's rejection of Jesus as Messiah. Secondly, an undeveloped category for inter-faith encounter is 'wisdom', which in the biblical tradition was clearly an international currency, with Israel borrowing from other cultures. In my own relations with members of different faiths I have often encountered a shared wisdom. Thirdly, we cannot escape the 'law of the cross': conflict cannot always be avoided. So long as the Christian faith embodies a prophetic concern for peace, justice and truth it cannot be embodied without anguish and without provoking some opposition. Needless to say, such conflict can divide Christians, who will often discover allies in other religious communities. The struggle against apartheid in South Africa offers one such example of both inter-religious co-operation and conflict within Christianity.

Fourthly, what we may properly aspire to as Christians is confidence rather than certainty. Confidence is compatible with my earlier acknowledgement of a place for perplexity; not so certainty. Thus, Rahner can insist that in the midst of perplexity 'we put our trust in God, and we are freed and consoled in all our needs and fears by the Holy Spirit. It is for this reason that Christianity is a message of joy, courage and unshakable confidence.'[46] Fifthly, the eschatological horizon – 'Love never ends . . . the partial will come to an end . . . Now we see in a mirror dimly, but then we shall see face to face. Now I know only in part, then I will know fully' (1 Cor. 13:8–10) – should encourage a proper reticence and hesitancy when we speak of the things of God, especially in inter-faith encounter. Finally – and this relates to the last point – we believe in a God of surprises. A revered mentor, Bishop Stephen Neill, used to delight in the following couplet: 'Beauty is God's surprise in nature,/The cross is God's surprise in revelation.' God has yet much to teach us (John 16:12–15). This will doubtless dismay some and excite others, as in the Early Church (Acts 10–11).[47]

Notes to Chapter 8

1 This title, which captures exactly the spirit in which I hope Christians will engage with members of other faiths, I have borrowed from Rowan Williams, *Open To Judgement: Sermons and Addresses* (London, DLT, 1994).

2 George Carey, 1996, 'The Challenges Facing Christian-Muslim Dialogue', *Islam & Christian-Muslim Relations*, 7:1, p. 98.

3 T. Modood, 'Racial Equality, Colour, Culture and Justice', the Commission on Social Justice, Issue Paper 5 (Institute for Public Policy Research, 1994), p. 3.

4 See Mark Juergensmeyer, *The New Cold War? Religious Nationalism Confronts the Secular State* (Oxford, University of California Press, 1993); G. Kepel, *The Revenge of God: The Resurgence of Islam, Judaism and Christianity in the Modern World* (Oxford, Polity Press, 1994); and Peter van der Veer, *Religious Nationalism: Hindus and Muslims in India* (London, University of California, Press, 1994).

5 *Is God a Virus? Genes, Culture and Religion* (London, SPCK, 1995).

6 *Jewish Chronicle* (25 March 1994).

7 See D. Cohn-Sherbok, *Issues in Contemporary Judaism* (London, Macmillan, 1991).

8 *Jewish Chronicle* (18 August 1995).

9 See S. Schwarzfuchs, *A Concise History of the Rabbinate* (Oxford, Blackwell, 1993)

10 *Jewish Chronicle* (7 July 1995).

11 Amos Oz, *Israel, Palestine and Peace* (London, Vintage, 1994), pp. 121–4.

12 J. Sacks, *Will We Have Jewish Grandchildren? Jewish Continuity and How to Achieve it* (Essex, Valentine Mitchell, 1994), p. 83.

13 T. Modood, 'British Asian Muslims and the Rushdie Affair', *Political Quarterly* 61:2 (1990), p. 145.

14 See E. R. Norman, *Anti-Catholicism in Victorian England* (London, Allen and Unwin, 1968) and S. Fielding, *Class and Ethnicity: Irish Catholics in England, 1880–1939* (Buckingham, Open University Press, 1993).

15 Eva Hoffman, *Lost in Translation: Life in a New Language* (London, Minerva, 1989), *passim.*

16 I have explored these issues in *Islamic Britain: Religion, Politics and Identity among British Muslims* (London, I. B. Tauris, 1994).

17 M. S. Raza, *Islam in Britain, Past, Present and Future* (Leicester, Volcano Press, 1991), pp. 32–3.

18 S. Akhtar, *A Faith For All Seasons: Islam and Western Modernity* (London, Bellew, 1990), *passim.*

19 H. Kureishi, *The Black Album* (London, Faber and Faber, 1995), p. 67.

20 *Jewish Chronicle* (7 July 1995).

21 See Robin Gill, *Moral Communities* (University of Exeter Press, 1992).

22 Grace Davie, *Religion in Britain since 1945: Believing without Belonging* (Oxford, Blackwell, 1994), p. 112.

23 A. Hastings, 'Church and State in a Pluralist Society' in his *The Shaping of Prophecy: Passion, Perception and Practicality* (London, Geoffrey Chapman, 1995), p. 117.

24 *Bradford Telegraph & Argus* (3 January 1991).

25 T. Modood, 'Establishment, Multiculturalism and British Citizenship', *Political Quarterly*, 65:1 (1994), pp. 53–73, *passim.*

26 J. Sacks, *The Persistence of Faith: Religion, Morality & Society in a Secular Age* (London, Weidenfeld and Nicolson, 1991), p. 68.

27 *Church Times* (12 June 1992).

28 I am indebted to I. Markham, *Plurality and Christian Ethics* (Cambridge, Cambridge University Press, 1994), for this last point.

29 See the Committee on Black Anglican Concerns, 'Seeds of Hope: Report of a Survey on combating Racism in the Dioceses of The Church of England' (London, the General Synod of the Church of England, 1991).

30 Michael Howard, *The Lessons of History* (Oxford, Oxford University Press, 1993), p. 150.

31 Peter Sedgwick (ed.), *God in the City: Essays and Reflections from the Archbishop of Canterbury's Urban Theology Group* (London, Mowbray, 1995).

32 D. Miller, *On Nationality* (Oxford, Clarendon Press, 1995), pp. 175–6.

33 K. Cracknell, *Justice, Courtesy and Love: Theologians and Missionaries Encountering World Religions, 1846–1914* (London, Epworth Press, 1995).

34 P. Hinchliff, *History, Tradition and Change; Church History and the Development of Doctrine* (London, Affirming Catholicism, 1993), p. 13.

35 A. Thistleton, *Interpreting God and the Postmodern Self: On Meaning, Manipulation and Promise* (Edinburgh, T. & T. Clark, 1995), p. 134.

36 D. Tracy, *The Analogical Imagination: Christian Theology and the Culture of Pluralism* (New York, Crossroad, 1981), p. 451.

37 Rowan Williams, 'Trinity and Pluralism', in Gavin D'Costa (ed.), *Christian Uniqueness Reconsidered: The Myth of a Pluralistic Theology of Religions* (New York, Orbis, 1990), pp. 11–12.

38 J. V. Taylor, *The Christlike God* (London, SCM, 1992), p. 245.

39 For the Hindu tradition see T. N. Madan, 'Secularism in its Place', in T. N. Madan (ed.), *Religion in India* (Delhi, Oxford University Press, 1994), pp. 394–409; for Islam, see P. Lewis, *Islamic Britain: Religion, Politics and Identity among British Muslims* (London, I. B. Tauris, 1994), pp. 126–7.

40 W. A. Meeks, *The Origins of Christian Morality: The First Two Centuries* (New Haven and London, Yale University Press, 1993), pp. 52–65.

41 R. A. Markus, *The End of Ancient Christianity* (Cambridge, Cambridge University Press, 1990), p. 134.

42 Tracy, *The Analogical Imagination*, op. cit., p. 451.

43 L. Newbigin, *The Gospel in a Pluralist Society* (London, SPCK, 1989), pp. 182–3.

44 Sedgwick, *God in the City*, op. cit., p. 24.

45 Karl Rahner, *Theological Investigations*, vol. XXII (London, Darton, Longman and Todd, 1991), p. 155.

46 Ibid., p. 160.

47 Most denominations now have a network of people with an inter-faith brief. There is also a Christian Interfaith Practitioners Association (CIPA). Information about these developments and appropriate contact people is available from Revd Canon Dr Christopher Lamb, secretary to the Churches' Commission for Inter-faith Relations, Church House, Great Smith Street, London SW1P 3NZ. The Interfaith Network for the United Kingdom, 5–7 Tavistock Place, London WC1H 9SS, can provide information about inter-faith groups and activities across the country.

Epilogue

Stephen Platten

'*Soundings* is the modest, perhaps over-diffident, title of a book that is noteworthy in more than one way and for more than one reason.'[1] So began Henry Chadwick's review of a book,[2] published in 1962, whose title inspired the title for this modest book of essays. The provenance of that earlier collection of essays is very different in many ways from the origins of this book. There the 11 essays were all written by Cambridge theologians who were or had been university teachers. In that sense there was a homogeneity about the collection that could not be claimed for this volume. *Soundings* issued from a group that had met together regularly for several years and who decided after 'some hesitation'[3] to collaborate in producing a set of essays. The essayists in this present book have met together as a group once only and then for a 24-hour overnight meeting. Admittedly, there are many established friendships within the group, but still the volume does not issue from a well-constituted homogeneous collection of authors.

However, we felt that there were sufficient resonances with *Soundings* for us to recall the title for those whose theological memories extend back that far. One of the resonances is well encapsulated a little later in Henry Chadwick's review, when he writes: 'The authors of the essays in this new volume do not advance a programme. They have not set out to compile a manifesto, and their words do not serve the interests of a particular party or platform in the Church of England.' That would be equally true of the authors' intentions in this volume. The intention is not to start a movement or theological pressure group. Nor is the book intended as a detailed and sustained reflection on the 'Tradition', using that word in a technical sense. Instead the intention is to reflect upon how Christian faith is handed on, and to see how such a process may remain faithful to the Christian past, while acknowledging the dynamic nature of 'tradition' in all its senses. This present time seemed an appropriate moment to 'take further soundings'. Debate about the nature of Christian theology and practice remains vigorous. It has not only been the ordination of women that has concentrated the mind. The Christian moral tradition remains at the centre of debate, as does the issue of inculturation. The waters remain as turbulent as they were in the 1960s, and the taking of soundings remains a challenging but essential task.

In retrospect, the 1960s were seen by many as a recrudescence of the spirit of the 'roaring twenties'. The precise landscape was not the same, but there was a similar sense of excitement and change. The 'swinging sixties' have now become legendary. Beatlemania, 'flower-power' and 'doing your own thing' characterised the decade. Politically it was a mixture of hope and despair. In Britain, Harold Macmillan heralded it with his declarations of the 'wind of change' in Africa and 'you've never had it so good' at home. On the world scene there was the hope characterised by the charismatic style of John F. Kennedy. This hope was dashed by his tragic death and the deepening crisis of the Vietnam war. Our introduction has hinted at a similar mood of ferment and excitement in theology. If John Robinson and Charles Davis characterised this on the more popular level, then 'Death of God theology' and the essays in *Soundings* raised the stakes within the more scholarly consciousness.

It is the subject-matter reviewed in the essays in *Soundings* which gives a clue to the essential issues that would come to the surface during that decade. Topics of fundamental theology remained central. The collection begins with an appeal to restore 'natural theology' to its central place within the Christian tradition. Interestingly enough, it was the banishment of that tradition from the theological stage by Karl Barth and other members of the neo-Orthodox school that ushered in the 'Death of God theologians' later in the same decade. This group of writers had been further influenced by Barth's exaggerated interpretation of the transcendence of God. Such extreme transcendence brought into question the relevance of God's existence to humanity. It is no coincidence, then, that G. F. Woods writes on 'The Idea of the Transcendent' in *Soundings*. In another essay by Woods the subject-matter is 'grounds of Christian moral judgements'. This is also partly the focus of Harry Williams' controversial essay on 'Theology and Self-Awareness'. At the heart of Williams' essay, however, is a plea for Christian theologians and pastors to come to terms with the work of Freud.

The whole volume is constructively critical in its approach. This is made plain in the essays on Christology, atonement and indeed prayer. The need for a continuing critical openness is further demonstrated in John Habgood's essay on 'Science and Religion' and Ninian Smart's contribution on 'Christianity and the Other Great Religions'. The relationship between science and religion was hardly a new subject for discussion, but fresh advances in scientific research sharpened the debate. The discovery of DNA, 'the double helix', by Watson and Crick in the 1950s was just one powerful example. The increased frequency and speed of world-wide travel had meant that encounter between the great religious traditions was now far more significant.

In identifying the climate of thought at the time, the essayists were doing more than simply heightening the awareness of theologians to the issues of the day. For such changes in intellectual consciousness extended well beyond the gothic window-frames of the university divinity schools. The influence of Freudian thought was contributing to a revolution in human self-understanding. The accelerating effects of the 'critical method' both in theology and elsewhere were perforce raising profound questions about the nature of authority in society. None of these questions has disappeared, and they have not left the Church immune to criticism and change. There were implications for the Church's self-understanding too. This is clear from all of the essays *implicitly*. In the final essay, however, Alec Vidler states the point *explicitly* too:

> Many of the religious elements in historic Christianity and much that has gone under the name of religion may thus be outgrown, or survive chiefly as venerable archaisms or as fairy stories for children, and we cannot tell in advance how they will be replaced or which of them will need to be replaced. We are at the beginning of a period in which we must be willing to prove all things and to hold fast only to what is good.[4]

Vidler picks up this insight and directs it sharply at the Church of England in particular:

> But our main question is: What prospect is there that the Church of England may have a continuing mission in a society where the traditional forms of religion are being outgrown? Does this church look like being able to welcome and foster new ways of discovering and nourishing the life in the Spirit?[5]

It would be comforting for some to believe that the Church of England uniquely has faced these challenges. That is not the case. All the mainstream churches have been challenged by these issues. Admittedly, they are posed even more sharply to churches that have a clear 'national role', such as the Church of Scotland, the Catholic Church in France and the Scandinavian Lutherans. All these questions have a familiar ring to them. Rather like a musical score set in rondo form, challenges to the churches to address society in a contemporary theological vernacular come round with a regular monotony. But they do so, as it were, in 'spiral rondo' form. Even if the questions appear to be set in precisely the same words, the nature of the engagement required is never quite the same. This realisation becomes particularly evident when one reviews this present collection of essays alongside those which comprise *Soundings*. It would be invidious to compare ourselves to that earlier august team, but it is not inappropriate to examine the contrasts between the issues of our day in relation to those identified by the writers of *Soundings*.

Perhaps the biggest single contrast is in Christianity's relationship to other religions. In Britain it was during the

1960s that large numbers of people continued to emigrate from Commonwealth countries and to make their homes in Britain. The large numbers arriving from the Indian sub-continent brought with them their own religion as well as their own culture. In the past 30 years Christians in this country have, for the first time, experienced living along-side substantial minority groups of Hindus and Muslims. This has challenged theological understandings. In the 1970s, John Hick, writing on the relationship between Christianity and other religions, spoke of 'The Copernican Revolution in Theology'.[6] Whether or not we accept his analysis, there is no doubting that there have been changes on the theological/sociological map. British society undoubtedly now exhibits greater religious and cultural variety than it did in the 1960s. Ninian Smart makes no reference to such variety in his *Soundings* essay; it simply did not exist. On two different occasions he writes: 'Let us transport ourselves in our imaginations to some Eastern country . . .' and then later, 'Journeying into foreign lands and alien cultures can bring one to a better understanding of one's own faith.'[7] Thirty years on, this all sounds slightly quaint. The theological questions posed by other religions cannot now be avoided, and those questions challenge the Church's self-understanding.

Jostling so closely with different religions and cultures is also bound to raise anthropological issues. In previous generations other cultures had to be observed at a distance; Margaret Mead travelled to the South Seas to find material for anthropological study. Now such differences are there on our doorstep. But anthropology presents challenges not only through racial and ethnic differences. Almost certainly the most profound shift here has been wrought through what is often described as the 'feminist revolution'. Trans-formed understandings of women and men have produced a series of different feminist theologies. The New Testament has been subjected to feminist theological analysis,[8] as indeed has systematic theology. The insights generated by feminist theology are a further challenge to the Church's self-understanding. It would be a gross over-simplification to see the ordination of women to the priesthood and episcopate purely in these terms, but undoubtedly both theological shifts and changes in ministerial patterns are affected by the feminist critique. Vidler and his co-authors could still happily use the noun 'man' to refer to humanity without any reader turning a theological hair.

What then are the questions that face us today? New Testament studies do not raise entirely different issues from those present 30 years ago, although the embracing of structuralist and other recent literary critical methods has increased the feeling of relativism caused by biblical studies. Indeed, certain schools of New Testament study have so sharpened their specialist tools of investigation that theologians in other areas of study have cynically ignored what they believe to be the increasing irrelevance of such fanciful techniques. Certainly in the world of historical theology, however, there has been a 'sea-change'. The critical methods long known in the laboratories of the scriptural analysts have now made their mark in what is described as 'doctrinal criticism'. The creeds and formularies of the Early Church have their own history and political background. Having been allowed an opportunity to glance behind the scenes, the drama will never now be viewed with quite the same naïveté. Similar reflection might be made about the liturgical revolution which has gained momentum since the Second Vatican Council. At the outset a historical purism dominated in liturgical study, but latterly there has been a developing interest in 'performative theology'. Imaginative liturgical study has led to a shift, away from 'common prayer' to produce something more of a supermarket culture. We continue to live in a world of liturgical booklets and song supplements.

It is difficult to assess, over the past 30 years, the precise changes in the relationship between science and theology. The impact of applied science has been extraordinary and has revolutionised people's lives. This may well have further distanced people from the immediacy of creation and thus of the significance of a divine Creator. This is not necessarily, however, a direct function of the relationship between science and religion, although the militant atheism exhibited by Richard Dawkins and others would argue for

195

this being the produce of a direct interaction between the two disciplines. Theology has continued to respond to the challenge of science and there has been a growth in interest in what might be described as a scientific and non-theistic metaphysic. The work of Stephen Hawking is the example *par excellence*. Interestingly enough, Hawking's *A Brief History of Time* is fast becoming (alongside the Bible) the best-selling and least read book on the market. The changes in this realm reflect some of the sociological evidence which indicates an increasing marginalisation of the institutional churches in the life of the nation. There seems to be a residual religious impulse, but it is less often mediated through or responded to by contact with the churches.

As Vidler pointed out so vividly in the early 1960s, changes in the intellectual climate produce immediate challenges to the Church's self-understanding. His final sentences put the challenge most sharply:

> Rather, its [the Church's] task is to represent, to stimulate and to defend all those agencies – however little ecclesiastical or religious they may be – that minister to the freedom and fullness of man's spiritual life.
>
> For the Church of England the great question is whether it can be transformed into such a church or is doomed to sink into the position of a religious denomination.[9]

This challenge remains as potent now (indeed more so) as it was then, and still more sharply applies to all the mainstream churches and not just the Church of England. Some of the changes described as having taken place over the past 30 years can easily induce a defensiveness which prompts the Church of God to define its boundaries more sharply. That is the first step on the road to increased sectarianism. But amongst all the changes described thus far, there is one prevailing tendency which should be identified and which potentially (for good or for ill) may have a significant effect upon the Church's self-understanding. It is the tendency toward fragmentation. This tendency will have an equal effect upon all the churches.

Almost all of the areas we have reviewed have this tendency latent within them. Specialism in theology can have a disintegrative effect upon the theological enterprise as a whole. Even within the theological community there has been confusion here. Systematic theology is often seen as a means of avoiding fragmentation. It is only capable, however, of integrating the great themes of Christian theology – salvation, Christology, eschatology, creation and so forth. The other disciplines of biblical studies, liturgy, moral theology and spirituality have a more subtle relationship with the doctrinal issues gathered together by the systematician. The pluralism of cultures born of recent immigration easily argues for a society where cultural and moral choice becomes a dogma and a necessity, undermining any common cultural mores. The political pressures towards the 'privatisation of morality' can easily encourage this process. Competing anthropologies and even liturgical diversity produce similar tendencies. Fragmentation often appears to encourage relativism and it becomes increasingly difficult for humanity to enter upon a process of self-reflection which can result in a holistic view of existence and experience. The search for meaning which lies at the heart of religion becomes increasingly difficult to sustain.

There is no denying what Louis MacNeice described as 'The drunkenness of things being various'.[10] There is undoubtedly a tendency within the universe towards increasing disorder; it is what scientists call entropy. Entropy is a term which issues from the Second Law of Thermodynamics and effectively describes the measure of disorder within a limited system at any point. It is a scientific fact that the natural tendency is towards an ever-increasing entropy. The amount of energy required to reverse the process, and thus to create integrity and order, is enormous. A simple practical example makes this clear. The energy and amount of work required to untidy a room is very considerably less than that required to restore it to order. This model might well be applied to the nature of our existence and theological reflection upon it. Our experience of the world tends towards increasing disorder; international conflict and disordered personal relationships are but two cases in point. The tenor of these essays, however,

197

is not one of pessimism or of a deterministic fatalism. Instead the theological endeavour is by implication integrative in nature. One of our essays argues explicitly in this direction and the implication is there throughout. This may be where the analogy of entropy, borrowed from science, breaks down or where it must be adapted radically. In other words, we are not simply arguing that 'more theological energy' will reverse the process of fragmentation described, or force things in a different direction.

Although these essays have engaged with natural science, social science and the humanities, there is a point beyond which these engagements must be transformed. Religion at its best will offer people a freedom and integrity which is not available from any other source. The spiritual director is not the same as a counsellor or a psychologist; the priest is not the same as a doctor or a social worker. Instead the Christian believer engages with each of these areas of human experience, but is pressed further toward a vision of life in its entirety as the gift of God. Integration is therefore not an option, it is a requirement of a theological view of the universe and of human experience. For the Christian theologian that requirement of integration becomes clear from reflection on at least three different levels. These three levels might be identified as a *reasoned theology of creation*, an *integrated approach to epistemology* and the *response to both of these in the ministry of the Church*.

Our contemporary experience does not make it as immediate as it was in past generations to dwell upon our *creatureliness*, or upon the gift of God's creation. Life in cities, and our increasing dependence upon technology can easily distance us from a clear perception of creation. The natural creation is now often mediated to us and received as 'second-hand' experience. Even life in rural areas is affected by the encroachments of urbanisation. It might be assumed that the 'scientific revolution' would make humanity marvel more at our creatureliness. In fact science does not automatically engender a sense of value, and Monod's rather bleak atheistic cosmology suggests as much.

Indeed, some of the great benefits of the scientific and

technological revolution tend to increase a human sense of isolation, dislocation and fragmentation. Television, for example, supports an isolationist culture; we do not need others to watch television. It is a solitary activity. If we are watching television it is irritating if others distract our attention. Computer games have a similar effect. Both of these activities again tend to mediate experience to us second-hand. An earlier sense of dependence upon the fertility of the land, and the kindness or otherwise of seasonal weather, led to a clearer perception of the responsibilities and sustaining powers of a Creator God. The Book of Common Prayer, for long the centre of devotion for Anglicans, included prayers for rain and fair weather and for use in periods of dearth or famine. But then, that book issued from a largely agrarian society.

A theology of creation requires us to see things 'whole' in a way which would not necessarily feel natural if we take for granted only mediated experience. In that sense theology works to decrease entropy or disorder in our perception of creation. It reminds us of our creatureliness, of our dependence upon one another for our well-being and survival, and ultimately of the fact that all experience is meaningless without a sense of God.

Moving from this fundamental level of a theology of creation, we might then ask a secondary-level question about *our knowledge of God and of the creation*. This has already been hinted at above in reflecting upon the creation itself. But alongside an epistemology of God rooted in the creation there is a broader issue of education and the search for truth. It is that question that underpins the perennial debate between a liberal education and vocational training. In earlier generations the balance almost always fell in the direction of a liberal education. The liberal education tradition emphasised education for the whole of human life. It assumed that there should be pursuit of truth for truth's sake and it avoided a narrow utilitarianism. Economic pressures have shifted the focus markedly toward vocational training.

Theological reflection drives us back in that direction in partnership with aesthetics. Art, music, poetry and drama have for long been closely associated with theological reflection. The churches and not least the cathedrals have been patrons of the arts. Preaching has often been seen to be allied with the poetic. Aesthetic and theological considerations, then, are closely allied and are integrative in offering a holistic approach to human experience. Ought we really to have offered these reflections in this book through the media of music, art, fiction, poetry and drama?

At the third level is our experience of the *ministry of the Church*. We noted that the spiritual director is not the same as the counsellor or psychologist, and that the priest is not the same as the doctor or social worker. When I was considering ordination, I was told by one whose counsel I valued: 'If you wish to work with people at the deepest possible level, where no aspect of human life and experience is excluded, then maybe you should consider ordination.' The point he made encapsulated great wisdom. The Church of God is the only institution which can offer to a fragmented society such an integrative vision.

In the inner suburbs of London – for example, in Kennington and Brixton in the south, or in Islington and Canonbury in the north – the fragmentation is very clear. Three or four distinct groups live alongside each other. There is a substantial poor black community, perhaps the majority. There is a working-class (and often ageing) white community. There is then sometimes an intellectual middle-class group which overflows into a gentrified professional community. Rarely do these communities engage with each other, except perhaps on a trivial level in the supermarket. It is only in church that there is any real sense of engagement.

Despite this, the pressure on clergy is to collude with the fragmentation they encounter. The unusual and integrative ministry of clergy does not seem to stand up alongside the professional and specialist training of the other caring professions. Clergy thus are easily frightened into seeking their own professional training as counsellors and psychotherapists. Even spiritual direction becomes a specialist option. The fact that often (and particularly in the inner city) the clergy are the only carers who live where they minister ought to be a reminder to them of their unique integrative role, and the fact that it is required of them through the theological foundations of the Christian faith. When national tragedies strike, it is often only the Church that can articulate the most profound feelings of the community. Clergy are called upon to bridge the gaps caused by society's fragmentation. So it was in the Scottish borders some years ago after the Lockerbie plane crash, and so it was later in Dunblane and with numerous other similar tragedies. The local minister or priest is called upon to reflect society's sense of loss and hope for a renewed wholeness.

The pressures upon the Church to conform to wider patterns of fragmentation should not be underestimated. To reverse entropy, to return to that scientific model, requires an enormous expenditure of energy. Within the Christian community, the pressures towards disorder and entropy are no less than those upon any other individual or group. They are no less within a theistic interpretation of creation. Presumably, however, talk of the power of the Spirit of God describes those energies which press toward integration and the restoration of order. It is that same power of the Spirit that, within the Christian tradition, has also been seen as the antidote for sin, the disordering of humanity's relationship with God. It was that same Spirit that was at the centre of God's activity in the Incarnation and in the transfiguration of suffering and death seen in the process of redemption in Christ.

Notes to Epilogue

1 Henry Chadwick, 'Soundings', *Theology*, Vol. LXV, Nov. 1962, No. 509, p. 41.
2 A. R. Vidler (ed.), *Soundings: Essays concerning Christian Understanding* (Cambridge, 1962).
3 Ibid., p. x.
4 Ibid., p. 254.
5 Ibid., pp. 255–6.
6 John Hick, *God and the Universe of Faiths* (London, 1973), pp. 120–32.
7 *Soundings*, op. cit., pp. 107, 121.

8 Sic, for example, the work of Elisabeth Schüssler Fiorenza, *In Memory of Her* (London, 1983), etc.
9 *Soundings*, op. cit., p. 263.
10 Louis MacNeice, 'Snow'.